KNOW
YOUR
BIRDS

KNOW
YOUR
BIRDS

Australia's Most Common Birds

Louise Egerton

First published in Australia in 2004 by
Reed New Holland
an imprint of New Holland Publishers (Australia) Pty Ltd
Sydney • Auckland • London • Cape Town
14 Aquatic Drive Frenchs Forest NSW 2086 Australia
218 Lake Road Northcote Auckland New Zealand
86 Edgware Road London W2 2EA United Kingdom
80 McKenzie Street Cape Town 8001 South Africa

Reprinted in 2005

National Library of Australia Cataloguing-in-Publication Data:

Egerton, Louise.
        Know your birds.

        Includes index.
        ISBN 1 877069 13 2.

        1. Birds - Australia - Identification. I. Title.

        598.0994

Project Editor: Yani Silvana
Designer: Joanne Buckley
Production: Kellie Matterson
Printer: Everbest Printing, China

Photo Credits

The majority of photographs for this book are derived from the New Holland Image Library.
Others were sourced as follows, according to page number:

Esther Beaton: 67, 127 top.
Bill Belson, Lochman Transparencies (LT):
    117.
Hans & Judy Beste, LT: 95 inset, 113, 139.
John Cooper: 47, 65, 85, 89, 105, 145, 165,
    171.
Jason Edwards, Bio-Images: 87 inset.
Ken Griffiths: 39, 71, 75 top and bottom, 77, 81,
    97, 103, 107, 123, 167 top & bottom, 169.
Jiri Lochman, LT: 19, 25, 37, 43, 55, 79 top,
    125, 127 bottom, 141, 159.

Stuart Miller, LT: 23.
Brian Nichols: 63.
Chris Ross: 91.
Raoul Slater, LT: 99, 101, 119.
Len Stewart, LT: 93.
Tom Tarrant: 115.
Geoff Taylor, LT: 41.
Klaus Uhlenhut: 87 main picture, 111, 137.
Dave Watts, LT: 17.
Cover images: Top right: Len Stewart, LT.
Bottom right: Ken Griffiths. Left: Raoul Slater, LT.

To the birds of Australia.
May they ever fly wild and free.

Acknowledgements

This book was 18 years in incubation but its hatching, when it came, was surprisingly swift and uncomplicated. However, I might have lost my nerve had it not been for the support of my friend, Punia Jeffreys. Rob Wall, too, was encouraging and made a number of constructive suggestions to improve the text. I am also grateful to his colleagues at the Cumberland Bird Observers' Club, Tony Saunders and Keith Brandwood who, in their scrutiny of a photograph, unmasked a White-browned Scrubwren impersonating a Brown Thornbill, or at least so it seemed to my amateur eye. Thank you to Darryl Jones, Senior Lecturer in Ecology at Griffith University, for enlightening me on how Brush Turkeys 'read' temperature. I am indebted to Nick Williams at the Australian Research Centre for Urban Ecology who kindly updated me on Red-whiskered Bulbuls in the Royal Botanic Gardens, Melbourne, and thank you Stephen Debus, author of *The Birds of Prey of Australia*, for giving me the benefit of your knowledge on raptor flight. Thank you, too, to the weather-smart Richard Whitaker for advising on meteorological fact versus folklore. To the hardworking team at New Holland, most especially Jo Buckley and Yani Silvana for their design and editorial expertise respectively, thank you both for helping to make this book what it is. Lastly, to my long-suffering partner, Fred Magro, whose patience and curiosity have allowed me to dawdle and watch the busy world of the bush without being hurried along, thank you.

Contents

INTRODUCTION 9

USEFUL WORDS 13

Introduction

This book is not for birchwatching experts. It's for people who look out of their windows day after day and see the same birds again and again and begin to wonder what they are. That is pretty much how we all get interested in birds in the first place.

Watch carefully and you will soon notice that birds have patterns of behaviour as distinct as our own. Like us, they are creatures of habit. The same bird often visits the same places every day. It might be a top look-out spot, a perfect insect hang-out, a nectar mecca or a cool shelter during the midday sun. Birds aren't stupid.

If you live in a unit, you'll still see plenty of birds. If you're on the eighth floor, you'll see different ones from those you'll encounter in the street. Stroll down to the local park and you'll see still more. Some birds live only by the sea; some inhabit lakes. Some are quite distinct, like the pelican, others are annoyingly similar on first inspection, like the Magpie and the currawong, or the Indian Myna and the Noisy Miner. The photographs in this book should help you recognise some of the birds you see every day.

If you can name a dozen birds after a couple of weeks of flicking through this book, you've done well. Of course, it gets easier, because whenever you see a new bird, you can discount those you already know, thereby narrowing the field. That, too, is the purpose of this book.

There are at least four wonderful books for identifying Australian birds but, with over 750 species living in or visiting the continent, these guides can be quite bewildering. Still more overwhelming are all the differences between males, females and juvenile birds. So *Know Your Birds* has narrowed down the field to the most common birds you are likely to see around our towns and cities.

I have tried to select birds that are either common everywhere or are extremely common in one city or another. Not everyone will agree with my selection and there may be a slight bias towards the eastern and southern coasts. But even if you're in Darwin, Hobart or Perth, you will find a great many familiar birds on these pages.

The order in which the birds appear in this book is based on similarities. Where birds look alike or are similar in some fundamental way they have been placed close together. So, for example, the terns and gulls, Starling and Blackbird, Silvereye and thornbills all appear next door to one another because they can be hard to tell apart. If you think you've identified a bird from the book, flick forwards and backwards from your choice just to check that there isn't another candidate with which it could be confused.

NAMING BIRDS

You may wonder why I have used capital letters for the names of birds sometimes and not at other times. The ones with capital letters refer to a specific species, for example the Pied Currawong. Names without capital letters, for example currawong, refer to all currawongs, of which there are three species.

Each of the 80 bird entries in this book may be about just one species, for example the Noisy Miner, or it may be about an identifiable group of birds, such as robins, honeyeaters or spoonbills. This is because some species are easy to identify, while others are very tricky, and when you are first learning about birds it is still extremely rewarding to be able to tell a robin from a thornbill or a rosella from a lorikeet, even if you cannot identify the species.

At the risk of incurring the wrath of the scientific community, I have sometimes taken issue with the common names. It seems to me that common names should be just that—names that are attributed by ordinary, non-scientific people. Often these are more descriptive than the conventional names. That there may be several different common names for a single species should come as no surprise, given that different groups of people, such as local farmers, traditional indigenous people and 'twitchers', may call them different things. I have chosen the names that I believe are most commonly used.

GARDENS FOR BIRDS

If you have a garden, you have a chance to encourage birds to visit and maybe even nest. Birds need places to live and sometimes we unwittingly destroy bird homes. If you want to encourage more birds to live around you, the best thing you can offer them is lots of different habitats for their different needs. Small bush birds like to hide in messy thickets. Honeyeaters and some parrots enjoy nectar-bearing flowers, such as grevilleas and bottlebrushes. The best habitat is multi-storey, that is tall trees (dead ones with hollows are highly sought after for nesting), dense high and low shrubs, thick grasses and groundcovers, and plenty of leaf litter. Birdbaths are extremely popular, too, in warm weather.

TO FEED OR NOT TO FEED

Feeding birds is not always a kind thing to do. They may become dependent on you, and an inappropriate diet can make birds sick. Rather than proffering food, the provision of shelter and water, especially in the summer heat, will entice a surprising number of birds into your garden. To lure still more, plant flower-, seed- and fruit-bearing plants, especially natives.

WHAT TO TAKE ON A BIRDWATCHING WALK

A notebook and pencil are essential for sketching the birds you see and their markings. Try to make your drawing and labelling as detailed as possible. Note the colouring of the crown, throat, breast, belly, rump and undertail coverts, as well as the back and wings. Often markings around the eyes will clinch identification down to species, especially in the case of the honeyeaters.

Of course, binoculars are invaluable if you have some. Always pinpoint your bird in relation to vegetation or landmarks first before putting your binoculars up to your eyes as binoculars immediately narrow the scope of your vision.

LOOKING AND LISTENING FOR BIRDS

For some species, choir practice starts at the crack of dawn. If you wake up at this time, lie in bed and see if you can identify the early birds by their calls. In the suburbs and on farms, kookaburras are often the first. Butcherbirds, Magpies and currawongs may follow soon after. In the cities it might be Willie Wagtails, Indian Mynas or pigeons. Birds usually have territories and these must be defended from encroachment by other birds. The early morning chorus is a declaration of ownership and a reinforcement of alliances.

The very best time to watch birds is just after day breaks, when birds are at their most active. Nectar is at its most prolific in the early morning, so for the nectar feeders, like honeyeaters, an early morning inspection of bushes will often yield a fine breakfast.

The middle of day is often the quietest on the bird front. In hot weather, birds retire to cool shady perches and attend to preening, snoozing or just waiting out the heat.

At dusk there is once more a flurry of activity. Flocking birds, like Starlings and Galahs, noisily congregate in tree branches in preparation for the night-time roosting.

On windy days look for bush birds in sheltered spots, as they don't like windy weather —it interferes with their ability to forage, fly and guard against predators.

FLEDGING INTO A BIRDWATCHER

As your interest in birds grows, you will begin teasing out the difference between species, even within some of the trickier bird groups. You will start to consult distribution maps that show the range of certain species. This is a great way of narrowing down your candidates. You will start to notice subtle colourings and markings. You will listen for calls. Through a series of enquiries, you may finally deduce that all the evidence points to one species. By that stage you will have moved on to using a pair of binoculars and one of the definitive field guides you will find listed at the back of this book.

I can only hope that *Know Your Birds* will be the first of many bird books that you will consult over time and that it will fire your curiosity to learn more.

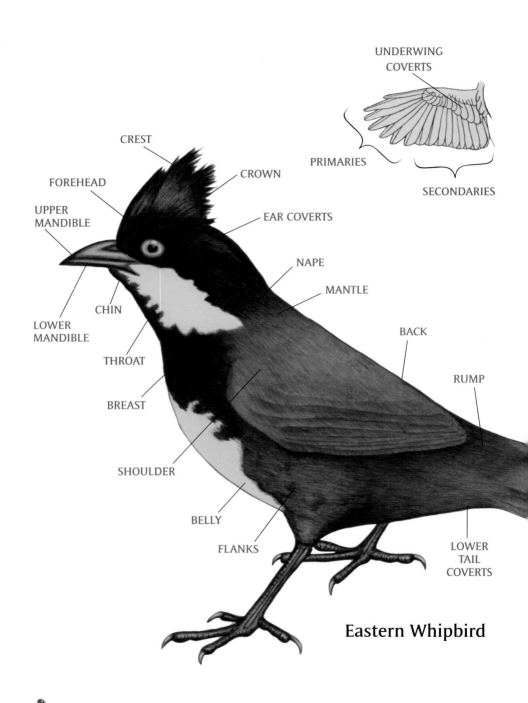

UNDERWING
COVERTS

PRIMARIES

SECONDARIES

CREST

FOREHEAD

CROWN

UPPER
MANDIBLE

EAR COVERTS

NAPE

MANTLE

CHIN

BACK

LOWER
MANDIBLE

THROAT

RUMP

BREAST

SHOULDER

BELLY

LOWER
TAIL
COVERTS

FLANKS

Eastern Whipbird

12

Useful Words

ACCLIMATISERS: In the 1860s Acclimatisation Societies became fashionable in Australia. Misguided members took it upon themselves to fill up parts of Australia with all sorts of animals, some from overseas but also native animals transported from one part of the country to another. Many of these introductions failed but we see the legacy of many others even today.

CARRION: Dead and rotten flesh.

COVERTS: Small feathers that cover the bases of larger ones on the tail and wings.

DABBLERS: Types of ducks and waterfowl that feed in shallow water on aquatic vegetation. They take floating weed from the surface or up-end to reach submerged plant food.

EYESHINE: The glint of eye colour caught in the beam of a torch.

FLEDGLING: A young partially or completely feathered bird still yet to fly.

GIZZARD: The muscular part of a bird's stomach that is lined with horny plates for grinding up food. Birds often swallow grit and pebbles to help in the grinding process.

GLEAN: To pick up food from various surfaces e.g. leaves, bark, branches or the ground.

INVERTEBRATES: Small animals without backbones. They are often insects but also worms, spiders, centipedes, snails, crabs, shrimps, mussels and lots of other tiny creatures. They make up the majority of animals on the planet but are not commonly seen because they are so small.

LBJs: Little Brown Jobs. There are a lot of small, nondescript birds that fall into this category and they are frustratingly difficult to identify. Birdwatchers, lost for a name, often refer to these birds as LBJs.

MIGRATORY: Undertaking regular seasonal flights between breeding and non-breeding grounds.

MONOTREME: Egg-laying mammal e.g. platypus.

MULGA: A type of wattle typically found in arid Australia: *Acacia aneura*.

NOMADIC: Undertaking irregular movements in response to environmental conditions e.g. rainfall.

SEDENTARY: Resident in a single area.

TAIL

TWITCHERS: Birdwatchers who keep a full list of all birds in an area, often a whole continent, and tick off the birds as they see them. The aim is to tick off every bird, so the rare ones become exceptionally prized. Twitchers may go to great lengths in order to see a rare bird.

Brush Turkey

70 cm

M any of us know this bird as a Bush Turkey. The first time you see one, it's hard to believe your eyes. Is it a real turkey, or a giant hen? Well, no and no. The real turkey that we are accustomed to eating for Christmas lunch is a domesticated bird that originated from a wild turkey that even today lives in densely timbered mountainous country of the eastern United States and Mexico. Australia's Brush Turkey remains thankfully wild and may very well have evolved here in the Southern Hemisphere.

Today Brush Turkeys are common around car parks and picnic grounds in many national parks, where there is thick wet forest and a substantial build-up of leaf litter. They have also started to invade the gardens and orchards bordering forests. They belong to a family called megapods. The 'mega' is Latin for big and the 'pod' for foot. They use their big feet to scratch through the leaf litter in search of invertebrates, fallen fruit and seeds.

The mega-feet are useful, too, for the extraordinary way in which Brush Turkeys incubate their eggs. Instead of sitting on them in the conventional manner, the male scratches up a gigantic mound of soil and moist leaves from the forest floor. It can take him up to two months, after which the mound may be 3–5 metres in diameter. Sometimes he renovates an old mound rather than start from scratch (ho! ho!).

Maintaining the right temperature in the mound is all important. It needs dense cover from the tree canopy to prevent the leaves from drying out. Just like a compost heap, it will then heat up, keeping the eggs warm. Brush Turkeys, sometimes known as Thermometer Birds, are able to gauge the temperature in the mound by 'tasting' a sample. Like chickens, it is believed that the roof of the bird's mouth, its palate, is highly sensitive to temperature. Just as a cook tastes for subtleties of flavour, so the Brush Turkey determines the thermal adequacy of its mound. When a female is drawn to the mound by the male's booming call, she tests the temperature herself to ensure it is suitable for egg laying before permitting the male to mate with her. She lays up to 50 eggs, but not necessarily all in the same mound, in an excavated hole in the top of the mound. She deposits them in layers, each layer receiving a covering of scratched-up sand, soil and leaf litter. She then walks away, never to return.

The male now undertakes the role of mound monitor. He will regularly test the heat of the mound: 34°C is the optimum temperature. If it is too hot, he will scratch away some of the fermenting leaves to reduce the temperature for the incubating eggs; if too cool, he will scratch more leaves up onto the mound.

One by one the chicks hatch and excavate their own way out of the mound. From day one they must fend for themselves. Such non-existent parental care is rare among birds.

Superb Lyrebird

80–100 cm

If you ever visit picnic grounds deep in the heart of wet forest where gullies of tree ferns or rainforest trees abound, you just may be treated to the sound or sight of a lyrebird.

The lyrebird's loud voice rings out through densely timbered country with such clarity and intensity that your sandwich may become suspended in mid-air en route to your mouth and your ears may pop out of your head in an effort to hear it again. You should not be disappointed as a lyrebird at full throttle is irrepressible. The song emanates from the male, who has learnt to mimic the sounds of his forest. He may be able to impersonate kookaburras, Magpies and Black-Cockatoos as well as less natural bush sounds, such as chainsaws and car alarms. With his extraordinary repertoire of songs the mature male advertises his prowess as a lover in the hope of drawing a female closer to his performance platform.

If you are drawn, as the female may be, to investigate further, you may come upon one of the most impressive sights in Australia's bird world. On or beside a huge mound of earth or on a low branch you will find a large, bulky bird bobbing up and down as he sings and fans out an astonishing tail bordered by a pair of impossibly long lyre-shaped feathers. If you're lucky enough to witness the complete courtship dance you will see him quivering his tail feathers and raising them up and over his entire body and head in a shivering display of unrivalled beauty.

Is it any wonder that females find him irresistible? During autumn and winter he will mate with as many females as possible. The male lyrebird does not concern himself with domestic duties so it is left to the females to gather twigs, bark and leaves and fashion them into a large, dome-shaped nest within a tree stump or rock crevice. And each female will raise her single young alone.

Lyrebirds don't fly much. They remain on or close to the floor of the forest where they literally scratch out a living with their big feet and strong legs searching through the leaf litter for ground-dwelling insects and other small creatures which they snap up with their sharply pointed bill. Sometimes the discreet little Pilotbird travels in the wake of these excavations, fossicking for leftovers. Although lyrebirds could be described as birds-of-paradise from relatively cool climates, they have no known ancestry beyond the Australian continent and they are believed to have evolved here. Once a bird only of the mainland, the Superb Lyrebird was introduced to Tasmania in the 1930s and 40s and its south-eastern distribution appears to be expanding.

The more obscure Albert's Lyrebird is restricted to the dense vegetation of gullies and rainforest on the Great Dividing Range around the New South Wales – Queensland border. It shares many characteristics with its relative but it is more colourful (chestnut) and has a shorter, less elaborate—though still impressive—tail.

Black-Cockatoos

Glossy: 48 cm
Yellow-tailed and Red-tailed: to 65 cm
Long-billed and Short-billed: 50–60 cm

It is hard not be impressed by the sheer size, blackness and elegance of these long-tailed birds as parties of them chart their course across the sky from one food source to another. Their flight is slow and graceful but many of their calls are loud ear-splitting screams which sometimes sound scratchy.

Black-cockatoos have especially well-developed upper mandibles. Like all parrots, their toes are arranged on their feet so two point forward and two point backward. This gives them the dexterity to pick up and hold woody fruits in one foot while prizing out seeds with their powerful bills. Stout bills are invaluable, too, for tearing open the holes and channels of wood-boring grubs and for peeling away bark to find insect larvae and spiders.

There are five species of black-cockatoo. Depending on where you see them, their size and the colour in their tails (and often their ear coverts), you can work out which one you're looking at. Probably the most common is the large Yellow-tailed Black-Cockatoo (opposite). This is the species you'll see in Tasmania and along the south and eastern coastal strip and ranges from eastern South Australia to central Queensland. The more northerly and inland range of the much rarer Red-tailed Black-Cockatoo overlaps with that of the Yellow-tailed Black-Cockatoo in northern New South Wales up to about Mackay. Inland it lives among woodlands, especially where they line watercourses, such as the Darling River. It, too, is large. The black body of females and young birds is flecked with yellow, while the male sports a substantial Elvis-like crest and red tail panels. Confusingly, in females and young birds the wing panels are usually orange or yellow.

Straddling the distribution of both of these cockatoos are the smaller Glossy Black-Cockatoos. These birds sometimes appear more dark brown than black. They have red tail panels. In females, these are edged with yellow; yellow is also sometimes visible around the neck and face. Glossies are specialist feeders, depending on the tiny seeds of she-oaks. Research into their declining populations is currently underway.

South-western Australia is home to two white-tailed black-cockatoos, both with white ear coverts. Their differences lie in the size of their bills and hence the food they can exploit. The tip of the heavy-duty top mandible of the Long-billed Black-Cockatoo is suited to extracting seeds from marri gumnuts, while the Short-billed Black-Cockatoo takes seeds from native bushes and introduced pines, and more often feeds on the ground.

In recent years, plantations of introduced radiata pine trees have begun to punctuate the Australian landscape. The flimsy seeds packed tightly into the cones of these pines seem to have met with approval from at least the Yellow-tailed and the Short-billed Black-Cockatoos. This may be the reason why we now sometimes hear and see these magnificent birds flying over the outer suburbs.

King-Parrot

43 cm

The sheer vibrancy of the male King-Parrot's livery is a once-seen, never-forgotten experience. His letterbox-red head, breast and underparts contrast with the bright forest green of his back and wings. You might also notice a small patch of paler green feathers in his wings. The female has a green back and red underparts, too, but her head and throat, to half way down her breast, are green. Juveniles are less colourful and have a brown, rather than a yellow, eye.

As their common name suggests, the demeanour of these striking birds is indeed regal. Unlike the squawking flocking cockatoos and squeaky lorikeets, they are sedate birds, restrained in their calls and in their behaviour. They inhabit the subtropical rainforests and tall eucalypt forests of the eastern seaboard. Here they seem to appreciate the coolness and deep shade of these wet forests and positively rejoice in their swirling mists and rainy downpours.

King-Parrots have a number of melodious calls: a soft peeping note, a joyous whistle and a conversational chattering that is almost human and consists of a mixture of soft peeps, whistles, churrings and chirrupings delivered at different speeds and tones. These 'conversations' seem to take place in the heat of the day under the shade of a thick canopy where they like to rest, preen and snooze.

Parrots are a faithful lot. When they pair off, it is usually a life-long partnership. To sustain the bond between them they take time out to give one another attention. They groom one another, engage in soft bill tussles, play tag up and down branches and from tree to tree and whistle and chatter to one another. Come the breeding season the male will court his partner as if for the first time.

The nest holes of King-Parrots are special. Ideally they are tall living trees, standing vertically and hollowed-out like gigantic didgeridoos. Their point of entrance must be high but the bottom of the nest can reach down almost to the ground. Here the pair raise as many as six youngsters in optimum conditions, but far fewer is usual.

Red-capped Parrot

This beautiful, brightly coloured parrot lives in only one part of the country, but for people living in south-western Australia, it is exceedingly common. For that reason, I have included it here.

Even on a short visit to Perth you should be able to find this quite big parrot. Try King's Park or, if you have transport and a day to spare, take a trip out from the city centre to visit Thomsons Lake Nature Reserve, a favourite hang-out for birdwatchers. If you are visiting Margaret River, you're sure to find it.

The Red-capped Parrot feeds on the ground but rests in trees and bushes for safety and shade. The adult plumage colouring of both sexes is almost unbelievable: a purplish blue breast, a red head and matching undertail coverts; bright yellow to lime green cheeks, throat and rump. Juveniles are duller and take time to acquire the full outfit, including the red cap. The bird's undulating flight, consisting of several fast wingbeats followed by a shallow glide, is distinctive and shows off its long tail. When perched, you should notice the wings, which compared with the tail are short; when spread you will see that they are also broad and rounded. Its scratchy voice is a crackling 'shrek'.

The Red-capped Parrot is a specialist feeder and its very limited distribution reflects the equally limited distribution of its favourite food—seeds from the locally common marri or red gum. Wherever there are marris, Red-caps abound. To extract the seeds from the urn-shaped fruits of this eucalypt the parrot has developed a long, hooked upper mandible that is tailor-made for the job.

Marris are often interspersed with other well-known Western Australian gums, such as wandoo, kauri and jarrah. The Red-caps will feed on the seeds of these and other native trees and shrubs. Fortunately marris provide good shade for stock and so they have often been spared the chainsaw in paddocks. Much to the frustration of orchardists, however, Red-caps have extended their menu to accommodate many of Western Australia's exotic fruits.

Ringneck Parrots

35–37 cm

There are no prizes for telling how to recognise these essentially green parrots. The yellow ring around the back of the neck is distinctive in all forms...of which there are no less than four. Each form has a separate common name. There is the Port Lincoln Parrot, the Twenty-eight Parrot, the Mallee Ringneck and the Cloncurry Parrot. Each has slight variations in their markings and lives in a different part of the mainland.

All the Ringnecks have long tails and relatively short wings. Their flight is swift, undulating and often close to the ground. They travel in small or large parties, feeding among the foliage of trees or on the ground. While seeds are their mainstay, leaf shoots and invertebrates living in vegetation and under bark are also taken. Their continual search for food means they are always on the move, and in outback areas they often follow tree-lined watercourses. They are dependent on tree hollows for nestings, even if trees are stunted.

As with all parrots, the males are more brilliantly and distinctly marked so, in order to clearly identify these four forms, look at the males. It's all down to the colour of their heads and the absence or presence of a small red band just above the bill.

Ringnecks are essentially parrots of the inland but their diet of dried seeds ties them to water. Even the widespread Port Lincoln Parrot, whose large populations roam the western and central parts of the inland, avoids the Nullarbor Plain and the Great Sandy Desert. You can distinguish Port Lincolns by their black heads...unless you're in the south-west corner.

The south-west corner is the stronghold of Twenty-eight Parrots (opposite). They, too, have black heads but the telltale red noseband just above the bill picks them out from their inland relatives.

Mallee Ringnecks have a green head and a red stripe above their bill. They occupy the vast inland tracts of south-eastern Australia up into southern Queensland, where populations begin to peter out around the Tropic of Capricorn.

Smaller, paler Cloncurry Parrots also have green heads but lack the red bill stripe. They appear to be an isolated population centred around Mount Isa but, as with all these forms, some interbreeding goes on, making identification difficult.

Many inland populations of parrots have taken a dive as a result of land clearing and the planting of 'improved' pastures but the Ringnecks have undoubtedly benefited from farmers sowing grain crops in sheets across the landscape. Probably only the lack of suitable nesting hollows restricts their growth.

■ Port Lincoln
□ Mallee
■ Cloncurry
■ Twenty-eight

Lorikeets

Rainbow and Red-collared: 28 cm
Purple-crowned and Little : 16 cm
Scaly-breasted: 23 cm
Varied: 19 cm
Musk: 22 cm

A suite of dazzling lorikeet species inhabit this continent, once known as the land of parrots. The one or ones you know best probably depends on where you live, but they all share certain characteristics: they are all noisy, gregarious parrots with long tapering tails and pointy wings capable of swift flight, often in large flocks. They commute each day from their roosts to flowering trees to feed on their staple diet of nectar and pollen.

If you get the chance, look at these birds' tongue. It actually consists of lots of closely packed spongey hairs that act as mops for soaking up nectar.

Most common along the east coast are Rainbow Lorikeets (opposite). They have become quite tame in many places where feeding tables beckon. Sometimes the Scaly-breasted Lorikeets join the Rainbows on their foraging sorties. You will be able to pick them out by their smaller size, green heads and the fringes of yellow on their green breast feathers, giving the breast a scaly appearance. In Darwin and northern Western Australia the Rainbow's distribution blends into the almost identical Red-collared Lorikeet, recognisable only by the band of red, or orange, across its nape and the almost black lower belly.

Red-collared
Rainbow

Musk Lorikeets, with a red-tipped black bill, a blue crown above a red forehead and a red 'teardrop' behind the eye, are the common lorikeets of Adelaide's suburbs.

Three smaller lorikeets are more often heard than seen in tree foliage. The tropical Varied Lorikeet, an inhabitant of Darwin's suburbs, has a pale pink breast, a red cap and yellow behind an eye ringed with white. The Purple-crowned Lorikeet is found in Perth. It has a beautiful pale blue front, a small purple crown above an orange forehead and large crimson patches under its wing. The discreet Little Lorikeet has a red face with a black bill. It prefers the treed open country of the east and south-east.

Varied
Purple-crowned
Little
overlap area

Lorikeet populations have increased over the last 20 years. Their bright plumage has endeared them to us and many of our crops supplement their staple diet. The outer suburbs of our cities and towns still provide enough eucalypts for food but tree nesting hollows are harder to find. Nevertheless, it is thought that lorikeets are displacing some of the rarer parrots.

Scaly-breasted
Musk
overlap area

Rosellas

At first sight you could be forgiven for mistaking a rosella for a lorikeet. Both are beautifully marked, relatively slender parrots of more or less the same size. However, rosella tails are longer, broader and more rounded; they do not taper down to a point as in the lorikeets. Another distinction is the rosella's trademark cheek patches; these are absent in lorikeets. Whether white, yellow or blue, they always stand out against the background plumage. If you're still not sure, look at the birds' backs. Those of rosellas are attired in two-tone feathers, the main colour fringed with a contrasting one to give a scalloped appearance. Last clue: the underwing coverts of all rosellas are blue.

Unlike the darting flight of lorikeets, the rosella's flight is more undulating and over shorter distances. It is hardly surprising that rosellas are more or less sedentary and that, rather than feeding in the tops of trees, they are mostly ground feeders, using trees and bushes for resting, preening, roosting, nests and shelter. Rosellas generally gather in pairs or small flocks. With their quiet demeanour and the camouflage afforded by the scalloping on their backs, they are often overlooked.

Today we recognise six species of rosellas, but their distributions rarely overlap. This sort of distribution pattern suggests the work of evolution. Seas or deserts can gradually arise over millions of years, driving what may become an uncrossable barrier through what once was a single ancestral species. Populations split in this way adapt to the prevailing conditions of their area and, again over time, eventually form separate species.

The two blue-cheeked rosellas almost certainly derived from the same ancestors. Most common in the wet forests of the south-east is the Crimson Rosella (opposite). The Green Rosella is endemic to Tasmania's eucalypt forests and woodlands. A form of the Crimson Rosella isolated by the Lofty Ranges and the southern Flinders River is the 'Adelaide' Rosella. It is an inhabitant of forested valleys, tree-lined waterways, roadsides and sometimes mallee. In coastal Adelaide and the surrounding hills its occurrence overlaps that of the white-cheeked Eastern Rosella. Another form of the Crimson Rosella, the 'Yellow' Rosella, inhabits the timber country of the Murray River in South Australia and Victoria.

In the white-cheeked group, the colourful, red-headed Eastern Rosella inhabits the treed farmlands and woodlands of south-eastern Australia. The white-cheeked Northern Rosella, with its black head and somewhat more restrained colouring, lives a more tropical existence in the paperbark swamps and open woodlands of northern Australia. The Pale-headed Rosella, with its lemony coloured head and red undertail coverts occupies similar habitat but through much of Queensland and northern New South Wales.

This leaves only the yellow-cheeked Western Rosella, which remains isolated in south-western Australia. This bird nests in the jarrah and karri forests and may also be found in wandoo woodland, where it often feeds on the ground among she-oaks.

Galah

35–37 cm

Galahs have a reputation for goofing around. Perhaps this is something to do with their playfulness after rain; what some people call their rain dance. Strictly speaking Galahs are birds of the hot, dry and dusty inland, where rain rarely falls. Is it any wonder then that Galahs celebrate the arrival of rain with agile acrobatics performed from tree branches and telegraph wires? Swinging upside down with wings akimbo they assist the raindrops to penetrate to the base of their inner feathers, especially in the crooks of their wings and under their tails, places where unwelcome parasites may lurk and cause discomfort.

Males and females are hard to tell apart, but the male's eye is a dark brown, almost black, while the female's is a reddish brown. Pairs bond for life and reinforce their commitment with regular, mutual preening and neck-rubbing sessions. Despite their long-term arrangement, males court their partners at the beginning of each breeding season.

Traditionally Galahs have inhabited the semi-arid woodlands of central and northern Australia. Although they take grass seeds, shoots and roots from the ground and the seeds of wattles from bushes, they need trees for nesting and water for drinking.

A Galah's nesting hole can be recognised by its bare entrance, the bark having been ripped away by the nesting couple. Theories abound as to why Galahs do this. Some believe it is a spring-cleaning job, removing the infested old bark to diminish the chance of disease in the nest. Others maintain it is a precaution against the predatory goanna, who loves nothing more than fresh eggs from tree hollows. It may also be useful nesting material. Certainly Galahs' nests are lined, sometimes with bark and often with leaves.

Galahs are long-lived birds. They may not breed in their first few years but reproduction rates tend to be high. The female lays up to 4 eggs and incubates them herself while the male keeps her plied with food. The chicks hatch in a month and, on drying out, they are already adorned with soft pink feathers. Once full fledged they will join a creche of fellow fledglings nearby. While they practise flying, take off and landing, their parents continue to visit them with food. Only when the last young bird has become proficient in flying will the whole family move off together to find good feeding grounds.

Ever since white settlement of the land, Galahs have been colonising new parts of Australia, discovering new sources of food in introduced weeds and cereal crops, and reliable water supplies in the form of farm dams. Populations have expanded dramatically. A map of the Galah's distribution 25 years ago would have excluded the whole of the eastern seaboard and Tasmania. Today it is common to see feeding flocks on grass verges anywhere in the well-watered parts of the mainland and now in Tasmania, where they are quite a common sight around Hobart and Launceston.

Sulphur-crested Cockatoo

45–51 cm

The Sulphur-crested Cockatoo is a noisy resident of forests and woodlands in the eastern half of Australia, including Tasmania, and in wooded areas of the Top End. Those around Perth are probably the progeny of birds taken from the east and raised as pets.

This cockatoo's magnificent yellow crest is forever on the move. The bird seems to raise it whenever it is excited which, judging by the frequency, is pretty often: when it alights on a perch, swings on a telegraph wire, inspects a nesting hollow or declares itself lord and master of all it surveys (or that's how it can seem). It even salutes the sun with it as the first rays warm its chilly breast, I am reliably informed by one human early riser. People have been pondering the relevance of birds' crests for some time. In the case of the Sulphur-crested Cockatoo it would appear to be serving a number of purposes. It certainly acts as a form of communication between members of its own species; it is probably a scare tactic to others; but on many occasions it seems like sheer exuberance. Certainly one time when you won't see a crest raised is when birds are feeding.

Although we associate these cockatoos with trees, and certainly they use them for roosting and nesting, they feed on the ground. They mostly stay in the same area and have a daily routine of flying in flocks each morning from their roosts to feeding grounds. As most of the flock feeds, several individuals position themselves high up on look-out posts and screech out raucous warnings if danger approaches. Through the heat of the day the flock rests in the cool shade of trees, amusing themselves by stripping the bark from the trees to unearth spiders and larvae. In the late afternoon they descend once more to the ground for a last feed before departing back to their roost en masse. Their staple foods are seeds, berries, flowers and nuts. Farmers complain that they rip open sacks of feed but they also keep weeds and locusts in check.

Male and female Sulphur-crested Cockatoos look alike but, if you're up close, you can tell the difference by the eye colour. The male has black eyes, while those of the female are reddish.

Corellas

Little and Western: 36–39 cm
Long-billed: 38–41 cm

Corellas are easily mistaken for Sulphur-crested Cockatoos (page 32). Both are essentially large, white, loud-voiced, squarky parrots that mostly travel in flocks. In flight the white plumage of both birds is flushed with a pale wash of yellow on the underside of the wings and tail. Corellas, however, are smaller and lack the yellow quiff-like crest. Their eyes are ringed with blue skin and there are often dabs of reddish pink between the eye and bill and under the chin on the throat.

While the more raucous Sulphurs are limited to wooded areas, corellas are traditionally inland birds that have expanded their range into the wheatbelt areas of Australia and more recently, driven by drought, they have forged their way towards the coasts. In these coastal towns and cities they have begun to catch our attention.

There are in fact three species of corellas. To distinguish them, you need to look closely at the bill and the flush of red on the face and throat. The Little Corella (opposite) looks very similar to, and is the same size as, the Western Corella. The 'little' perhaps refers to its bill, which is small compared with the very long and pointed upper mandible of its western counterpart. You may also notice a wash of red between the blue eye-ring and bill. This facial coloration is stronger and more extensive on the Western Corella. The Long-billed Corella also has an oversized upper mandible and its red facial feathers are matched by a red patch on the throat. Distribution, too, can be critical in determining species, but for Perthsiders, teasing out the subtleties of identity will be most challenging, as all three species may be found in their city.

Like Sulphurs, they are seed-eaters, although the long-billed species also dig up plant roots. Despite trapping by the pet industry and shooting by farmers, corellas have proliferated due to the presence of seed crops and metres of feedlot troughs, together with a ready supply of water from dams and bores. Probably only the shortage of nesting hollows in trees restricts their population growth. The Long-billed Corella has not been thwarted in even this respect: it has been known to excavate nests in the ground and to have bred in the holes of quarries and cliffs.

Little
overlap with Western

Long-billed

Black-shouldered Kite 33–37 cm

It may have black shoulders but the first thing you'll notice about this bird of prey is that it's white. If you've ever travelled on a country road and looked up at the telegraph wires running alongside, you might have noticed a rather sleek, more or less white, hawk.

Black-shouldered Kites are the most common medium-sized birds of prey in mainland Australia. They inhabit sparsely wooded grasslands. Paddocks cleared of all but a few trees are ideal. The grass verges alongside roads, considerably kept in check by council workers, are favourite hunting haunts and telegraph wires make ideal watchtowers. From here they can beadily watch for the stirrings of rodents below. Once located, they will glide down into position and hover with upswept wings and depressed tail as they lower their legs before dropping like a stone for the kill. Birds, reptiles and insects in the grasslands are also all vulnerable to these aerial attacks.

The only other white hawk in Australia is the Letter-winged Kite, a rare, mostly noctural inland bird. It, too, is exceptionally fond of rodents but it concentrates more on the nightlife. Occasionally the hunting hours of both kites overlap and in places like the Channel Country and Barkly Tablelands of Queensland, where Letter-winged Kites are relatively common, there may be some confusion.

At rest both white kites have black shoulders and in flight, both have long pointy wings (unlike the larger kites whose outer wing feathers are spread like those of eagles). When airborne, however, the patterning on the underwings is quite different. The Black-shouldered Kite has black wing tips, while the Letter-winged Kite earns its name from the very distinct black M- or W-shaped marking outlined against its pale undercarriage.

Birds of prey are vulnerable to poisoning. Being at the end of the food chain they can accumulate loads of toxins from the food they eat...enough to kill them. In attempts to control mouse and rat plagues farmers often unwittingly poison both these kites. Pesticides also knock down populations of hawks. Ironically these birds are wonderful pest controllers in their own right. In a plague of mice, rats or locusts, left unhurt, they will breed up a storm and in so doing reduce pest populations.

White-bellied Sea-Eagle

Males: 75 cm
Females: 85 cm

It is an uplifting experience to see an adult White-bellied Sea-Eagle gliding effortlessly along the tideline of a beach and, for those living near the sea, rivers or lakes, not an entirely uncommon one. These beautiful birds are quite abundant throughout most of their range, although there appear to be fewer in South Australia.

First and foremost this is a fishing eagle. It is proficient at flying low across water, bringing its legs down like the wheels on an aircraft. At first it projects them forward, then it perfectly breaks the water's surface to grasp its wriggling prey. An adult can take large muscular fish, and with powerful shallow beats, despite its load, once again attain height. It carries its thrashing prey to the nearest safe perch either for immediate dismemberment and consumption or for ongoing transportation to the nest.

White-bellied Sea-Eagles actually have quite an extensive menu. They take a lot of seabirds and can ably pluck an exhausted Little Penguin (page 158) from the water. They raid the nests of terns and gulls, harass other birds to drop their prey, and snatch perched birds from trees. They eat sea snakes, rabbits and carrion.

The clean contrast of dark grey and white plumage is the trademark of the adult Sea-eagle. In flight, you see white underwing coverts and body, and dark grey primaries and secondaries. Looking at the bird at rest, you see a pristine white head, breast and belly with dark grey wings. Confusingly, however, young birds take up to four years to attain adult plumage. Before that they are brown and can be hard to tell from juvenile Wedge-tailed Eagles (page 42) but generally their plumage is less rich in colour and streaked with cream. With maturity they become increasingly pale and more like their parents.

A good guide for identifying birds of prey is the length of the tail in relation to its wings. This Sea-Eagle's tail, although wedge-shaped, is very short and the wings when folded may reach beyond it, unlike in Wedge-tailed Eagles. Sea-Eagles also lack the full-'trousered' legs of the Wedgies, whose legs are feathered right down to their feet.

White-bellied Sea-Eagles do not breed until they have their adult plumage. Ideally, they prefer to nest in large trees directly beside lakes or rivers, or on vertical cliff-faces. Either way they usually command a good view. On the Great Barrier Reef, however, the best a Sea-Eagle can hope for is a sturdy *Pisonia* tree. On the offshore islands of Western Australia, pairs may have to build on bare ground. Nests are not unlike those of Wedge-tailed Eagles, consisting of piles of sticks which, over years of use, accumulate to become huge stacks up to 2 metres in diameter and sometimes almost as deep.

Brahminy Kite

45–51 cm

In many tropical parts of the world, where the water meets the land, Brahminy Kites can be seen soaring gracefully on warm air currents. Around the northerly coasts of Australia, this bird cruises the still waters of estuaries, mudflats, bays, islands and quiet shallow sandy coastlines with spits. The mangroves are perhaps some of its best hunting grounds.

Its pure white head, mantle and breast contrasting with a rich chestnut-coloured body are unmistakable. In flight you will notice its short tail and broad, black-tipped, almost horizontal wings. Compared with the White-bellied Sea-Eagle (previous page), its feet, toes and talons are weak and incapable of grasping or lifting very heavy prey.

Less adapted than the White-bellied Sea-Eagle to the challenges of strong coastal winds, the Brahminy Kite spends more time sitting beside water than on the wing. From a well-hidden perch it watches and waits for food to come its way. A common haunt is a well-camouflaged branch in mangrove swamps, where the rhythmic tide sweeps in and retreats, leaving fresh food stranded and exposed to the kite's gaze. While fish make up the majority of the Brahminy Kite's diet, frogs, snakes and crabs are all literally up for grabs. They can also snatch small birds and insects in mid-air or airlift them from the water's surface or tree canopy. They also scavenge for food in the harbours and towns of Australia's northern coasts, taking advantage of the dropped and rejected food of humans, and they will feed on carrion.

Brahminy pairs usually build their nest out on the horizontal limb of a tree overhanging water. They may make a fresh one each year or restore a delapidated one that has been ravaged by moonsoonal rains. Sticks are collected to make a platform and the centre is lined with leaves, seaweed or soft man-made materials. In the tropics, birds breed during the Dry but further south they usually begin nest-building in late winter in time for feeding their one or two young with the bounty of spring.

Wedge-tailed Eagle

Males: 90 cm
Females: 100 cm

Of all the birds of prey in the Australian skies, Wedge-tailed Eagles are the largest and they soar above their territory from dizzy heights. This macro-level hunting is very different from, say, the close-up hovering of the Nankeen Kestrel (page 46) or the Black-shouldered Kite (page 36). Masters of the air currents, Wedgies spend much of their life airborne. With folded wings, they can plunge hundreds of metres and recover the height effortlessly by outstretching their wings once more and skilfully catching an upsurge of air. Good timing, precise movements and subtle adjustments of wing and tail feathers are the key to this energy-saving strategy of sky riding and diving.

Like all birds of prey, Wedgies grab their prey with their large, curved talons. Just a flex of the feet draws these deep into the flesh of their victim. In so doing, internal organs may be punctured, the injury quick and fatal.

Birds of prey are difficult to identify because so often we only see them in flight. With the sun in your eyes, the bird's silhouette against the bright sky may be all you have to go on. Recognising the silhouettes of birds of prey therefore is a skill all of its own. Luckily the Wedgie is one of the easiest to identify, partly because of its sheer size. When soaring, its wings are upswept and the feathers at the end of the wings (primaries) are clearly spread out like fingers. The tail is indeed wedge-shaped, being decidedly narrower at its base. The smaller of a pair is the male and the darker one is the older. Old Wedgies can be almost black; young ones are a rich honey brown and bear a golden mantle across their shoulders.

A Wedge-tailed Eagle's nest is a wonder to behold. High up on the limb of a large tree, a massive collection of dead, broken branches are piled up to a spread of maybe 2 metres in diameter. Wedgies usually have several nests in their territory and rotate breeding between them. Sometimes a nest is taken out of commission by a chainsaw, termite attack or a lightning strike. Each year the parents will raise one or two chicks. Once fledged, they will spend a couple of weeks flapping their wings at the nest, lifting off a metre or so in practice for their first flight. In eight months they will have learnt all they can from their parents and be expected to move on to establish their own territories.

It is rather shocking to know that until 1974 it was permitted to shoot these magnificent animals. They remain at risk from poisoning from the 1080 bait so commonly laid down for their prey. Ironically, the intervention of humans has also inadvertently benefited these birds. Rabbits are probably their number-one food item and roadkill carcasses, especially on outback highways, are another important food source for adults.

A Tasmanian subspecies of the Wedge-tailed Eagle is in great danger of being wiped out by land clearance, loss of nesting sites and persecution.

Whistling Kite

51–58 cm

This is not an easy kite to recognise on its looks alone, but the first thing to catch your attention is likely to be its cry: a clear descending whistle chased by several ascending staccato notes. If you hear such a sound, look for its source; you may be rewarded with the sight of this large brown bird of prey. You may notice the long, rounded tail and the bow-shaped angle of its wings as they beat slowly and deliberately, the ends spread out like fingers. The undercarriage is a paler brown than the upper surface. When perched or at rest on the ground, use a pair of binoculars to make out the faint crest of head feathers that gives it a slightly scruffy look.

Whistling Kites are common and widespread throughout most of Australia, except in Tasmania, where they are rare, and in the inhospitable dry centre of Western Australia, where they have yet to be recorded. The bird owes its survival to its ability to adapt. For example, it can live in many different types of habitat. It is often seen around estuaries, lakes and rivers but will live and breed even in desert regions. In fact, in a year that brings good rains, the breeding populations in desert regions may outnumber those on the coast.

It is flexible, too, in its diet. It does hunt and take live prey, including fish, from just beneath the water's surface but, like most kites, it is primarily a scavenger. It will take insects, rodents, birds, reptiles and even the birth placenta of domestic stock. Carrion also forms part of its diet and several birds may converge to feed on a large roadkill.

For a nesting site, Whistling Kites are likely to pick the tallest tree they can find within suitable habitat. Sometimes they give an old nest a makeover, tidying up and adding to the stick construction and adding a new lining of fresh leaves. While winter and early spring nesting is favoured in the well-watered areas of the south-east and virtually any time seems OK further north, wet conditions at any time are likely to be the prompt for nesting in dry inland regions.

44

Nankeen Kestrel

30–35 cm

Other hawks can, and do, hover but none can hover with the dexterity and precision of a kestrel. Even in a roaring gale, a kestrel can hang in the air on a single spot. This is no mean feat. Balance in the air is sustained by the coordination of wing and tail movements and requires delicate and constant adjustment to keep pace with the unpredictable gusts and lulls of the wind.

Although kestrels often hunt from a high vantage point, such as a tree branch, telegraph wire, rock-face or fence post, hovering is their speciality and it provides some distinct advantages. It gives the kestrel a close-up view of the ground, enabling it to scan it for prey. Once pinpointed, it hasn't far to drop before making contact with outstretched talons.

Being a small hawk, prey, too, is relatively small. Grasshoppers perhaps form its staple food but spiders, skinks, mice and even small birds are all on the menu. Like most hawks that hunt on land, it likes open country, where prey can be easily detected, with scattered trees or other lookouts from which to survey the ground for movement. Rarely does a kestrel take prey on the wing, although it is not unknown.

Common in all parts of Australia except Tasmania, where sightings are rare, this bird's small size, hovering flight and unusual colouration set it apart from other Australian birds of prey.

Its common name, Nankeen, is derived from Nanking, a city in China renowned for the production of its beautiful fabric. The colouring and patterning on this kestrel's back and upper wings are reminiscent of the cloth. In contrast to this pinkish brown colouring, its underparts are pale, almost white, and the wing tips are black. Black bars on a chestnut tail distinguish the female from the unbarred, grey-tailed male. However, a broad black band at the end of the tail, tipped with white, is common to both.

Australian kestrels don't bother to build a nest. They either use an abandoned one of suitable size, or nest in the hollow spout of a tree limb, in a crevice or on the ledge of a rock-face. Nesting begins in early spring and the female does most of the incubation while the male feeds her. After a month the chicks hatch. Within a further month the young have moulted two downy coats and, fully fledged in almost adult plumage, they are able to leave the nest. The parents will continue to feed them until they have learnt to hunt for themselves.

Boobook

The Boobook may be the commonest owl in Australia but, being nocturnal, it's not easy to see. It is very often heard, however, and its call, once known, is unmistakable. It is just two notes uttered close together again and again: 'boo-book' or, if you are familiar with the European cuckoo, you could say 'cuck-oo'. Some people know this bird as a Mopoke, another name derived from its call.

You might wonder how any animal can hope to catch a fast-moving mouse or antechinus on a dark night. Certainly some light is useful and probably an owl's best hunting is done during twilight and under a full moon, or even a street light, but owls are superbly equipped for night hunting and a life of stealth. Their enormous eyes gather as much light as possible and their retina contains a battery of receptors for detecting shapes and, more importantly, movement of shapes. They also have a neck joint that allows them to silently rotate their head 180° or more, thereby avoiding disruptive body movements that might alert prey to the owl's presence. Acute hearing is another asset. The flattish face, edged by a ruff of short, hair-like feathers, forms a perfect receptor for gathering soundwaves and funnelling them to the ears. Silent flight, too, is invaluable.

The Boobook might look endearing to us but a nocturnal victim might have a very different point of view. Once prey is located, the Boobook swoops down with not a whisper of sound and spreads its wings over the ground to block escape. The talons dig into the animal's flesh—three forward, one back—and lift it off the ground and up to a perch for consumption.

Owls, unlike other birds of prey, swallow their prey whole. They have a very efficient gizzard which mashes all parts of an animal to a pulp and separates out the inedible fur, feathers and bones. These are regurgitated as hard, dry, tightly-packed food pellets. Sometimes you can find these under a large tree, a sure indication that owls are using it. If you also see splats of white poo, this may be further confirmation that a branch above serves as an owl's roost or perch.

If you want to see a Boobook, your best chance is to go out with a friend into a well-timbered area at night and scour the branches of gum trees with a torch or spotlight for eyeshine when the bird calls.

Tawny Frogmouth

The Tawny Frogmouth is not an owl, despite its owl-like appearance and its nocturnal habits. It is found throughout Australia in wooded suburbs with mature trees. In the bush, it lives in woodlands, forests and along tree-lined watercourses.

It is an exciting bird to discover as it is quite large and impressive. In leafy suburbs at night, you might make out the bulky outline of one perched on a wire, fence or washing line. Or you might just get lucky and catch sight of one in the glow of a street light. Frogmouths appreciate street lights. Not only do they cast light on the ground, which is where frogmouths mostly hunt, but they attract moths to the light. Frogmouths are not averse to a supper of hawked moths and it makes for an easy meal. They will also hunt for food among the branches and leaves of trees. Most of their fare, however, comprises nocturnal ground-dwellers: insects, mammals, birds and reptiles—in fact just about anything provided it is small enough to swallow whole.

The Tawny Frogmouth has a spooky call, a deep resonant 'oom, oom, oom' that repeats over and over, bringing a haunted primodial quality to the night. Like the owls, the flight of the frogmouth is silent. The most usual hunting tactic is rather like that of the daytime kookaburra: watch, wait and pounce. While their feet are weak, their mouth is exceptionally wide and the bill is hooked. The arrangement of long bristles around its mouth may be a device for netting prey that might otherwise have made good its escape.

There is one other way of seeing a frogmouth and that is during the day. Frogmouths roost in trees and their cryptic plumage provides superb camouflage (males are generally greyer and females browner). When they feel threatened, they adopt a curious pose which makes them virtually undetectable to all but the most practised eye. They stretch their chin up into the air, close their eyes and assume a stiff, vertical posture that passes very convincingly for the broken limb of a tree (see above).

Laughing Kookaburra 42–47 cm

Here is a bird we all know and love, but how much do we know about its lifestyle? Have you noticed how kookas seem to hang around in groups? The members of these groups are all family.

A pair of breeding kookaburras requires a large woodland territory, about 5 hectares. They need tall trees, a suitable nesting hollow, dense areas for cover, particularly for the young, and open ground for hunting. Water is a bonus. Although kookas belong to the kingfisher family, they are well adapted to dry-land hunting.

Enlisting last year's offspring as helpers in defence of their extensive territory provides them with a team of babysitters and food fetchers for next year's brood. Establishing new territories with sufficient food and suitable nesting hollows is a hard call, and first-year offspring benefit from sharing their parents' territory in return for some hard work.

Kookaburras pair for life but each year the male will court his 'wife' with food titbits and undertake the excavation of a nest hollow or remodel an old one. Sometimes the damaged wall of an old termite nest can be hollowed out to become suitable. The pair share the incubation of the eggs with their helpers. When the young hatch, they're naked and blind but plied with food from day one by an endless stream of family visitors.

With exceptionally keen eyesight and a powerful bill, kookaburras are fine marksmen. Watch one hunting in the wind from a swinging perch—a spindly branch or telephone wire—and you may notice how the bird's body swings with its perch but its head remains stock still and its focus on the ground beneath unbroken. The hunting tactic of the kooka is watch, wait and pounce. If it moves, it's lunch. Snakes, lizards, mice, insects and spiders are all on the menu. So are baby birds.

The family members of a territory reinforce its boundaries morning and night with their rumblings, chortlings and outright deafening cackling choruses. The signals are loud and clear but there are a couple of invaders who are not easily dissuaded. Goannas are probably the greatest threat to nesting kookaburras. Proficient tree climbers, they are very fond of eggs and small birds. Birds of prey, too, are a worry. At these critical times, the family works as a team to bombard the trespassers and expel them from the territory. Success calls for a volley of loud celebratory cackling.

The Laughing Kookaburra lives only in Australia. It was originally a feature of the eastern seaboard and ranges. Not so long ago a rarity in Tasmania, it is now common in the north and east. It was also introduced into Western Australia by the acclimatisers of the 1890s and is now quite common in the south-western corner of the State. There is also a Blue-winged Kookaburra that inhabits New Guinea and the woodlands of northern Australia.

Feral Pigeon

About 33 cm

This, the common street pigeon, is probably the best known and most despised bird in Australia. It is hard to miss in the busy heart of any of our major cities, including Darwin. Yet somehow its familiarity makes it almost invisible to us. When they are noticed, Feral Pigeons are generally frowned upon. They are accused of fouling public buildings, blocking drains with their nesting material and generally being dirty.

In fact these pigeons have served human beings extremely well. Their association with us goes back to way before the time of Christ, Mohammed or Buddha. Their other, less damning common name of Rock Dove is derived from their descendants, who once lived on cliff ledges and in caves of the North African coast. Rock Doves are recorded as having been domesticated and bred by the Egyptians for food 3000 years ago. They have also been used as messengers throughout the ages.

Humans have continued to breed pigeons through the centuries and they have been an invaluable source of food, especially to the people of the Northern Hemisphere through the bitter fallow days of winter. Their remarkable ability to find their way home to the place where they hatched has led to breeding by pigeon fanciers, who race them from rooftops, providing both sport and an opportunity for city-bound humans to touch on the lives of another species. Ironically, today these birds are extinct from their land of origin.

Our Feral Pigeons very probably came over with the First Fleet, along with the cattle, sheep and grain, as a reminder of home, for game and for eating. Here, as all over the world, this bird has adapted to the rigours of life on the streets. Once a seed-eater, it now gleans food from rubbish bins, and roosts and nests on the ledges of buildings. Despite the hazards of living among humans, these pigeons can breed up a storm. They attain sexual maturity at six months and they can raise a brood of chicks in only a couple of months.

With all this breeding going on over the centuries, there has been inevitable hybridisation, resulting in a mixture of colour variations. However, most Feral Pigeons are still shades of light and darker grey, usually with some white, and most bear a pink noseband and an iridescent green and mauve mantle over the neck.

54

Peaceful Dove

About 20 cm

The words 'pigeon' and 'dove' have derived from two different languages but they are more or less interchangable. Generally speaking, however, a dove is considered to be smaller than a pigeon. The Peaceful Dove is indeed a relatively small, slender and long-tailed pigeon with a quiet unassuming demeanour that suits its common name well.

The Peaceful Dove's plumage is also unassuming and not unlike a number of other small, long-tailed pigeons. The clue to its identity lies in the delicate dark bars over the pinkish buff breast feathers and the blue ring around its eyes. The Laughing Turtle-Dove (page 58), a common resident of Perth with which it is sometimes confused, is an altogether more reddish bird. The Bar-shouldered Dove, which shares residency with the Peaceful Dove in Darwin, is heavily barred on the back, wings and neck but lacks barring on its front.

Although not a particularly striking-looking pigeon, the Peaceful Dove has a number of calls by which you might recognise it. A distinctive, clear 'doodle-doo', often heard throughout the days of summer, underscores its seemingly gentle nature. Sometimes you will also hear a quite different deep, reverberating gurgling that probably signals alarm. When courting, the male reverts to soft seductive coo-ing.

Not all birds need to drink. Those that feed on flesh and berries may be able to derive enough moisture from their food to do without access to water but the seed-eaters, such as finches, parrots and pigeons, need fresh water to survive. That is why this little pigeon, despite its ability to live in the dry, hot inland, must stay reasonably close to water. Unlike most birds, pigeons can suck up water directly without having to take sips and then throw back their head to swallow. Pigeons of desert regions have a drinking routine: arriving at sunrise and sunset each day, they immerse their beaks into the water and drink deeply.

Pigeons have a storage sack at the bottom of their oesophagus in which they can stockpile food, a handy adaptation for a bird whose food supply can be plentiful but patchy. This storage sack, known as a crop, has another very remarkable function in pigeons. It can produce something known as pigeon's milk. Only pigeons, and a few of the world's parrots, are able to feed their young directly from their own bodies like mammals do. The 'milk' is nutritious and has a high fat content, which is derived from the breakdown of the parent's own internal cells.

Peaceful Doves may feed on the ground but they roost and nest in shrubs and trees. They have adapted well to living close to humans and many lead sedentary lives in our cities today.

Turtle-Doves

Spotted: 27–28 cm
Laughing: 24–27 cm

The turtle-doves are a group of pigeons that live in the tropical and warm-temperate parts of the world. They have long, attenuated tails and can be recognised by their distinctive neck patches. Only two species are found in Australia and neither are native. The Spotted Turtle-Dove (opposite) and the Laughing Turtle-Dove were introduced into zoos: Adelaide and Perth respectively. Both became escapologists and today Laughing Turtle-Doves thrive in south-western Australia; some have followed the railway line up to Kalgoorlie and established there. Spotted Turtle-Doves continue to do well along the coast east from Adelaide and up the eastern seaboard. A small contingent—the result of later releases—continues to breed in Perth.

The back and wings of the Laughing Turtle-Dove are a rusty orange except for the bluish shoulders. Its head and breast are flushed pink. Its most distinctive feature is a throat patch, a rusty crescent marked with black dashes. The head and breast of the Spotted Turtle-Dove are similarly flushed pink but the wings and back are essentially brown and this time the neck marking is a handsome polka-dotted white-on-black collar over the nape.

You may have noticed that male pigeons put a lot of time and effort into courting females. The turtle-doves are no exception. Not only do males bow, coo, strut and pirouette around their apparently nonchalant partners, they also perform acrobatic flights in an effort to impress them. These consist of flying high up into the air, then, with wings held high, freefalling out of the sky in a fast dare-devil swoop.

For a nest, like all pigeons, turtle-doves build a rather untidy platform of twigs only sunken enough to prevent the two eggs rolling out. Unlike some of the more threatened native species that nest on the ground, these nests are stashed into dense bushes, the thick foliage of low trees, or sometimes the hollows of buildings.

Australia's two turtle-doves have established well in the parks and gardens of our towns and cities. Traditionally grain eaters, they have followed the human grain trail, and spread into rural areas, taking advantage of our messy habits, our plantations and the infestation of weeds in disturbed areas. The challenge of finding food beyond cultivated and inhabited areas has, fortunately for native birds, not yet been met.

Spotted
Laughing
overlap

Crested Pigeon

31–35 cm

The finely honed point of this pigeon's crest suggests hair gel. Impossibly long and vertical, it is the bird's trademark. Only the much smaller rusty-coloured Spinifex Pigeon of rocky outcrops and spinifex country in the west and north of outback Australia can boast such a fine crest. The overall plumage colours of the Crested Pigeon are muted: soft greys on the head, neck and breast, with a flush of pink on the shoulders and fawn on the back and tail. Apparent at close range are the red eye-rings, matching legs and the dark scalloping on the wings, interrupted by a striking patch of iridescent purple, orange and green.

In the same way that some people can whistle through a gap in their teeth, the Crested Pigeon can whistle through a gap in its wings. This gap is due to a couple of shorter-than-usual feathers in its outer wings; this allows air to pass between the full-length feathers as it flies.

Like most pigeons, the Crested Pigeon bobs its head as it walks. In fact what it is doing is keeping its head as still as possible for as long as possible in order to keep a steady eye on what's happening on the ground in the food department. Eventually its head must catch up with its body, which it does with a single quick jerk.

Crested Pigeons used to be inland birds. They mainly feed on dry seeds but in remote areas they supplement this diet with the shoots and leaves of native medick plants, which are widespread throughout the outback. They have benefited enormously from the importation of grains onto farms and rural properties have also supplied them with their other vital ingredient for life: water.

Gradually, this adaptable species of open spaces has migrated, first into country towns and now into the suburbs of many mainland cities. Pairs and loose flocks are often seen feeding along roadsides. It is probable that clearing and the proliferation of grassland-type weeds here and beneath powerlines have acted as highways to migration into and out of human centres. Only the wet-forested regions seem to be out of bounds for this essentially dry-country bird.

Wattlebirds

Little: 26–33 cm
Red: 31–39 cm
Yellow: 38–48 cm

Once you can recognise some of the most common birds in gardens and parks, it's time to stretch your identification skills to the wattlebirds. A good size, they are common in the cities and towns of southern Australia provided you know where to look.

Wattlebirds are large honeyeaters and, like most honeyeaters, their major food source is the nectar of native flowers. In the bush, they roam forests, woodlands and heathlands for flowering trees and shrubs. They will come into gardens and feed along the edges of bowling greens, playing fields and golf courses wherever there are extensive plantings of large flowering natives. They are very vocal birds and their harsh croaky calls are meant to be heard by all in the vicinity. They are usually declarations of territorial ownership and are easy to recognise once you are familiar with them. In fact, you often hear these noisy individuals before you see them.

Once you've located your wattlebird, and provided you live on the mainland, you have two species to choose between: the Red Wattlebird and the Little Wattlebird. Both are quite common. Generally speaking, the larger, longer tailed Red Wattlebird inhabits higher vegetation, often lording it over extensive living bouquets of gum flowers or perhaps a bottlebrush tree. Most distinctive is the long red wattle of skin that hangs down from the sides of its head like dangling earrings. These grow longer with age.

The plainer, more subtly marked Little Wattlebird lacks the more pronounced streaking, reddish eye and yellow flush on the belly of male (and some female) Red Wattlebirds, but the flash of orange in its wings helps identify it. Because this bird is especially fond of banksia flowers, it can often be seen in heathlands and coastal scrubs. Some authorities now classify the western form of the Little Wattlebird, which specialises in dryandras as well as banksias, as a separate species and they call the eastern form Brush Wattlebird after the brush tongue common to all honeyeaters.

Where there's nectar, you'll find wattlebirds. Take a walk through heathland in winter, when many plants are in flower, and you're bound to hear the Little Wattlebird's harsh grating cackles and defiant 'quok'. Among flowering eucalypts you'll hear the trumpeting 'chock, chock, chock' of the Red Wattlebird.

Tasmania's Yellow Wattlebird is the largest of them all. It visits suburban gardens and orchards and lives in eucalypt woodlands, dry forests and heathlands. It defends its feeding patches with harsh guttural gurgling sounds. Its bright orange or yellow wattles are unmistakable and distinguish it from the Little Wattlebird.

Red
Yellow

Little

Friarbirds

Little: 25–30 cm
Noisy: 30–35 cm
Silver-crowned: 28–32 cm
Helmeted: 32–36 cm

It is the loud raucous voices of these aggressive squabblers arguing in the canopy of flowering trees that usually catches our attention first. Their clattering, clucking and crowing is interspersed with more pleasant ringing tones in some species. Although these honeyeaters mostly rove about in small flocks searching for nectar, they seem to spend as much time chasing off other contenders for the nectar as they do feeding. They also take insects and visit orchards and wineries.

The sight of a large friarbird is enough to make a small bird fall off its branch. Of the four species, only the Little Friarbird looks even remotely friendly. The other three have a thuggish appearance, largely due their partly or wholly unfeathered black head studded with a reddish eye. Most daunting of all is the pronounced knob on the top of the stout, curved bill. Although they have the body of a large honeyeater—pale grey or buff on the underside and dark grey or brown above—they resemble a miniature vulture.

The widespread and knobless Little Friarbird scours the trees of woodlands, pastures, swamps, mangroves, parks and gardens for blossoms. It has a bare blue patch beneath the eye that extends to its bill. You can tell the juvenile by its yellow-tinted throat.

The name 'leatherhead', often applied to friarbirds, is most suited to the larger Noisy Friarbird (opposite), as its whole head is bare black skin (save for a thin eyebrow of pale bristles), giving it a sinister appearance. Its pale grey breast plumage is lightly splayed out like a feathery bib and the darker feathers on its nape sometimes stick out untidily. It shares much of the Little Friarbird's territory and visits heathlands when banksias are in flower.

The Silver-crowned Friarbird of northern Australia has a subtle 'bib' of feathers too but, apart from its quite different range, it has a silvery smooth-feathered crown. The larger Helmeted Friarbird has a more buff-coloured feathered crown extending to a 'helmet' of tufted feathers at the nape. One form lives in north-eastern Queensland; another lives on the Arnhem Land escarpment.

Friarbirds usually suspend a woven cup of bark and grass, bound with spider webs and lined with fine roots, from a horizontal fork in the outer branches of trees 2–20 metres high, well camouflaged by foliage. Nests built in flowering gums provide convenient food supplies close to home.

Helmeted

Little

Silver-crowned
Noisy
overlap area

Whipbirds

Eastern: 25–30 cm
Western: 20–25 cm

Although the Eastern Whipbird is hard to see, its call is one of the most distinctive sounds of dense bushland. Once learnt, it is never forgotten and it is fun working out which is the male and which the female. From a thicket of tangled understorey scrub, the male draws out a sweet, clear note before exploding into a short, sharp, loud crack of the whip. There are no prizes for working out how the whipbird has earned its name. Sometimes, if the smaller female is present, she will chase up the whipcrack with two short notes: 'choo-choo'.

The Eastern Whipbird (opposite) leads a sheltered life under the protection of a messy spread of strewn branches in gullies and wet forests. It also resides in the gullies and rain-forest remnants of small reserves around homes in the suburbs of many eastern cities and towns. In areas disturbed by the activities of humans, vegetation often consists of small-leaved privet, lantana and other smothering weeds. Here they remain mostly hidden from our gaze. At best we may glimpse the pointy black crest and a black and white face attached to a relatively large olive brown body skulking around in the bushes.

Safe from predators, whipbirds forage for insects among the leaf litter and glean food from branches and leaves. They also take seeds. If these prove difficult to extract from their pods or husks, they can lean back on their tail and 'knees' and use their feet like hands to hold the receptacle as they peck away to reach the objects of their desire.

The day-to-day activities of courtship, territorial defence and nesting are conducted in their netherworld of understorey bushes. If breeding is successful, a pair of whipbirds will raise two youngsters; occasionally they will try for a second brood in a season. Like the birds themselves, nests are well camouflaged, the outer edges looking like little more than a jumble of balled vegetation. The inside however becomes increasingly neat and well formed, with soft dry grasses lining a cup.

The smaller, rarer Western Whipbird takes a lot of finding. It inhabits much drier heathlands, mallee country and even spinifex grasslands in distinct areas of South Australia and Western Australia. Its call consists of four scratchy notes, followed by a pert three from the female. Even in the right places and habitats Western Whipbirds are elusive, their olive green crowns and heads providing even better camouflage than the black of their eastern counterparts.

Eastern
Western

Red-whiskered Bulbul   23 cm

The long, pointy crest of the Red-whiskered Bulbul leaves no doubt as to this bird's identity. Like a dunce's cap, it sticks up vertically into the air. On closer inspection you will see an equally distinctive dab of red feathers behind each eye and a thin black line separating a white cheek patch from a white throat. A red undertail is also distinctive.

This bulbul belongs to a family of over 100 species that live throughout Asia and Africa. They are melodious singers and many of the more attractive species have long been associated with humans as caged birds, although tropical forests and their edges are their traditional homes.

In Australia, the Red-whiskered Bulbul does not stray far from human habitation. Introduced from south-eastern Asia at the turn of the nineteenth century, it has established itself well in Sydney and around Coffs Harbour. In Adelaide introduced populations died out and in Melbourne reports from the botanic gardens and the parks around South Yarra suggest it continues to hang on, but not in numbers.

Bulbuls are active, alert and vocal birds, found mostly in gardens, parks and waste-lands. They eat invertebrates, berries, soft fruit, shoots and buds. From a perch on a high point overlooking an expanse of open ground, their loud fluid songs declare ownership of territory. Such perches also provide a good lookout from which to hawk for insects.

They nest in spring and summer. The nest, a cup of roots, leaves and bark bound together, is well hidden in the foliage of shrubs, vines and low trees. Here the female will lay two to four white eggs blotched red–brown.

Unlike so many of our introduced species, this bird appears to have established in Australia without upsetting the balance of things too much. However, there is concern that because it feeds on the fruits of such weed species as privet and lantana it is spreading their seeds into natural bushland, thereby reducing native vegetation and so the habitats of native animals. In addition, its taste for fruit and buds might pose some risk to gardeners and orchardists were it ever to breed up in large numbers. However, given its record in Australia for the first hundred or so years, this seems unlikely.

Willie Wagtail

About 20 cm

As they swivel their tails from side to side like demented battery-driven toys, these little black and white birds certainly get your attention. This distracting behaviour is usually performed from a perch a metre or so above the ground and accompanied by high-pitched, slightly grating volleys that are undoubtedly alarm calls. Perhaps this is a necessary temperament and an occupational hazard in a flycatcher, since flycatching obviously requires quick reactions and acute observational powers.

You are most likely to encounter Willie Wagtails on nature strips and playing fields, where they spend much of their time hawking flies. They have an endearing habit of accompanying you as you walk over grass. Don't be fooled though. They're not after your company. They follow you because as you carelessly walk along you disturb insects in the grass which the wagtail can then intercept in mid-air before they have the chance to land. Willie Wagtails belong to the fantail family and share the family characteristic of indeed fanning their tails, and often their wings, in an effort to net flying insects.

These birds live happily wherever there are perches and flies to catch, even in the inner suburbs. Through spring and summer, they sing sweet trilling songs for hours on end, especially at first light and even through the night. The relaxed fluid song contrasts utterly with the bird's alarm call.

The seemingly innocuous Willie Wagtail is in fact an intrepid mobster of large birds. In particular, the kookaburra gives the wagtail a lot of cause for concern during the breeding season. Knowing the kookaburra's taste for small nestlings and its skills as a hunter, the wagtail defends its territory by wrecking its adversary's concentration with tireless screeching and repeated attempts at knocking the kookaburra off its perch. It often wins, the annoyed hunter leaving for easier pickings.

Even more astounding are stories of Willie Wagtails nesting in the base of eagles' nests. Given the Willie Wagtail's wariness, it may serve the nesting eagle well to have a live-in sentinel to give the alarm call at the approach of any danger. The Willie Wagtail, on the other hand, may remain unbothered by other predatory birds while under the protection of such a giant.

Finches

F ew of us have enough enticing long grass in our backyards to attract finches—unless we allow our lawn to go to seed. But look around the unkept edges of parks and playing fields or the reed and sedgebeds of lakes, keeping your ears tuned for the twittering conversations of small birds, and you may locate a flock of finches busily feeding.

Ideally suited to a life among grasses, you can always pick a finch by the shape of its body and bill. The dumpy little body, relatively short tail and small size enables it to manoeuvre through vertical thickets of grasses manageably. All finches are seed-eaters, although insects, which are usually plentiful during the breeding season and while raising young, are often taken. The short, stout bill is strong enough to split open seeds, yet finely pointed to act as tweezers for picking up small seeds.

Most finches travel in flocks. Being small birds, they are vulnerable to attack by large ones and travelling in numbers provides protection. Members of the flock keep in touch with constant contact calls. If you see a flock, stop and watch how they move together across terrain, calling all the while to keep the stragglers from trailing behind.

Their nests are domes fashioned from grass, and the eggs laid within are always white. Because the eggs are always safely hidden in the dome nest, there is no need for them to be camouflaged with colour like those of some other birds with more open nests.

Wherever there are grasslands in the world, there are finches. In Australia, we have 20 or more species. Several roam the inland areas but never far from water. In all but the wetter coastal regions of mainland Australia, you may come across Zebra Finches. These little red-billed finches, with their barred black and white tails, get their name from the male's chin and breast markings. While the female is essentially pale grey and brown, the male bears prominent chestnut patches beneath his eyes and on his flanks; those on the flanks are spotted with white.

Other species have very resticted distributions, such as the Blue-faced Finch that inhabits the tropical high-altitude forests of northern Queensland or the tiny Red-eared Finch, endemic to Australia's south-western corner. The Top End is especially well endowed with finch species. Around Darwin alone you may hope to see at least three species.

Finches with red rumps are known as firetails. On the east coast, from Cape York around to southern South Australia, the most commonly seen firetail is the Red-browed Finch (opposite). Populations of this species also exist around the Perth area, completely isolated from their eastern counterparts. Red-browed Finches have adapted well to the new grasses introduced into Australia by farmers and landcarers. However, other native finches do not favour exotic grasses so much and have fared less well.

House Sparrow

15 cm

The House Sparrow has sustained a close relationship with humans for 6000 years. This historical association goes back to when humans first settled down to sow seed and farm the land. The sparrow was introduced to Australia from England in the 1860s.

Sparrows belong to the finch family. You can see the resemblance in the size and shape of their body and bill. And like finches (page 72), seeds are their major source of food. So is it any wonder that when humans began storing seed to plant and to feed their livestock, sparrows cottoned on?

Today the barns and yards of eastern Australia remain sparrow strongholds. They have learned to adapt to eating more than just seeds. The fruits of orchards, restaurants, gardens and parks are now to their taste. So, too, are the small buds of many plants. Handouts at bird feeders are enthusiastically welcomed. As if the food alone were not a compelling reason to stick around, humans have unwittingly supplied sparrows with a plethora of sheltered, predator-free nesting sites in the eaves of their buildings.

These sociable birds hop along the ground and through bushes and trees in foraging flocks, keeping in touch with one another with animated chirrupings and chirpings. Come spring, flocks break up and males (opposite, above) court females (opposite, below) by bowing, spreading out their wings and lifting their chin to sing in front of nesting holes they have already selected in culverts, bushes, hollows or buildings. At such times homesteads and outhouses may be abuzz with the twitterings of nesting couples as they gather dried grass and sometimes paper and fabric before lining the rather untidy ball of a nest with soft feathers.

Another species, the Tree Sparrow, was imported into Australia at around the same time as the House Sparrow. It has only a limited distribution, in Victoria and southern New South Wales. Male and female Tree Sparrows both look very similar to the male House Sparrow, and since they often travel in the same feeding flocks, they are hard to tell apart. The telltale clues are the chestnut, rather than grey, crown and a dark smudge on the white cheek.

House Sparrows are breeding up rapidly in eastern Australia and they are aggressively muscling in on the best real estate, sometimes even evicting native birds from their own nests. So far they have remained contained within the eastern half of the continent but Western Australian authorities remain vigilant. Ironically, while House Sparrows are gaining new territory in Australia, populations in England are plummeting.

Pardalotes

Spotted: 8–9 cm
Striated: 9–11 cm
Red-browed: 10–12 cm
Forty-spotted: 9–10 cm

When you earn your living hanging upside down prising sticky lerps off the undersides of gum leaves high in the trees, a long tail is something of a liability. Perhaps this explains why pardalotes barely have one. Psyllids are tiny insects that suck sap out of leaves and branches, especially the undersides of young juicy leaves at the end of new shoots, where they construct soft, dome-shaped, sticky shelters (called lerps) for themselves. The pardalote's short blunt bill is perfect for dislodging these, but to reach the outer limits of the canopy it must also be light and small, and to hang on upside down while feeding, its legs and feet must be strong.

It's not easy to find pardalotes. You could give yourself a serious crick in the neck looking for them unless you start with a clue—their continuous soft pipping calls. Raise your eyes skyward and scan the canopy for movement. You may see several little birds moving methodically through the foliage of one tree, before moving on to the next. If you have a pair of binoculars you will be able to make out their beautiful bright colours and see how industriously they work over the undersides of young leaves.

There are four species of these pretty little birds in Australia. On the mainland you are most likely to see either the widespread Striated or the Spotted Pardalote. The Spotted (opposite) displays white spots on a black background on both its crown and wings. A red rump and a yellow throat are also distinguishable. Its call is a two-syllable 'wee-wee'. That of the Striated is more often a three-syllable 'wee-diddup'. It lacks the spots but has a black and white streaked crown and a brownish olive back. A red spot on the wings is often evident and bright yellow on its breast, flank and eyebrow is clearly visible.

In dry, more remote country, Red-browed Padalotes scout for lerps on the gum trees lining watercourses. Where gum trees are rare, they will take their dinner from the underside of mulga leaves. The rare Forty-spotted Pardalote lives only in some dry sclerophyll forests of south-eastern Tasmania and on Flinders, Maria and Bruny islands.

There's another reason why a pardalote needs strong legs and feet. Perhaps surprisingly, this little bird nests by excavating a tunnel in an earthen bank, often beside a road or creek. At its end the pardalote scrapes away a nesting chamber, which it lines with bark and grass to make it cosy for the young chicks. It's dark in the chamber so the young chicks have little glow-in-the-dark patches on either side of their gape that guide their parents to their mouths when they arrive with morsels of food in the gloom of the hole.

If you are really lucky, you may locate a pair of nesting pardalotes in bushland near your home or even in your garden.

Spotted only

Fairy-wrens

12–15 cm

Poking up from a pert little body, the fairy-wren's tail is unmistakable. These small birds live under the constant threat of detection by predators such as large birds and cats. They generally feed on the ground, staying close to dense cover at all times and flying low between bushes. Fairy-wrens live and move around in groups. When not breeding, they may join other species, such as pardalotes (page 76) and thornbills (page 82), in mixed feeding flocks. Larger groups may flush out otherwise overlooked food items and provide greater protection, thereby allowing more time for feeding.

In the breeding season, fairy-wrens form pairs but sometimes the breeding pair is attended by other fairy-wrens. These are often last season's offspring that have stayed in the territory, but sometimes they are new members that have migrated into the group. Most bird species are unprepared to tolerate the presence of other sexually mature birds in their breeding territory, but fairy-wrens are an exception.

In fact, researchers have studied the breeding behaviour of Australia's fairy-wrens in some detail and discovered that they have a quite complex social organisation. They refer to fairy-wrens as 'cooperative breeders'. This means that within a breeding territory, while only one male and one female are dominant, others are permitted to remain and to help in the feeding of the young and protection of the nest.

While such breeding behaviour is not unknown in other parts of the world, it is rare. Yet in Australia cooperative breeding behaviour has been recorded for a number of species. Why this should be so is a hot topic for bird ecologists. Perhaps cooperative breeding is a way of regulating populations? We know that fairy-wrens can modify the size of their clutch according to the bounty of a season. And we know that nearly half the eggs fairy-wrens lay do not make it to fledglings (many are probably taken by currawongs—see page 172). Non-breeding helpers feeding the young and undertaking sentinel duties must undoubtedly contribute to the breeding success of the dominant pair. Perhaps their success outweighs the disadvantages for those who don't get to breed.

How you look is important in the fairy-wren world. Only the dominant male will wear the full breeding livery (see male Superb Fairy-wren, opposite above). Other attendant males may display slight touches of breeding plumage but they will not breed in the group unless the dominant male dies. Female fairy-wrens (see Superb Fairy Wren, opposite below) typically remain discreetly plumaged all year round.

Once upon a time fairy-wrens were common in gardens and parks but in recent years they have disappeared from all but the more unkempt bushy places. Surveys show that small garden birds are on the decline in our built-up areas. The opening up of spaces previously dense enough to shelter fairy-wrens has the double-edged effect of inviting in their predators, such as the beady-eyed currawongs.

Silvereye

These busy little birds are continually on the move. Being small and vulnerable to attack by large predatory birds, they travel in flocks under the cover of thick bushes or leafy canopies. In such parties they operate as a team, sweeping host plants free of insects, picking ripe fruit and mopping up nectar, before moving on to the neighbours. Although insects are their mainstay, they have a brush-tipped tongue rather like that of the honeyeaters for soaking up nectar . They are as fond of lantana fruits as of any native fruits, and for this proclivity they have been blamed for spreading weeds into the bush in their droppings.

Silvereyes are naturally wary so if you want to see them be prepared to stay still in a single spot for a while and wait for them to come to you. A continuous spread of shrubs in a relatively open area is good place to choose. As with fairy-wrens (page 78), Silvereyes could once be found in any messy backyard with overground shrubs but the recent trend towards turning gardens into tidy outside rooms has not been conducive to much wildlife, and certainly not to Silvereyes. Today's makeovers of former city garden habitats are much more to the liking of Noisy Miners (page 98). However, the scrubby areas of large city parks or coastal dunes are still visited by Silvereyes and if you find one, you're bound to find more. You'll hear their rapid high-pitched notes as they stay in touch with one another and you'll be able to track them down by sound, as well as sight, as one in the group zips out of one bush into the next to be followed by the crowd.

Silvereyes have a nomadic lifestyle chasing the food supply. In all but western populations, they also migrate seasonally. In spring and summer, they suspend small cup-shaped nests of tiny twigs and grass from the outer leaves and branches of bushes. They usually lay three pale blue eggs, and three weeks after hatching the youngsters are fledged. After breeding, they gather into large flocks and move northwards.

Tasmanian Silvereyes fly over the Bass Strait by night, an impressive undertaking for such small birds. If you happen to see a Silvereye with orange to buff flanks during winter on the mainland you have just spotted one of these intrepid travellers. At winter's end, the migration pattern is reversed.

Thornbills

Thornbills are the classic little brown jobs or LBJs. Since they are all small and more or less brown, the 12 species are hard to tell apart. However, once you get your eye in, it's quite easy to recognise a thornbill by its tiny size, rounded body and slender, dark bill that seems tailor-made for picking up small insects, although thornbills do take small seeds as well.

To avoid direct competition with other thornbills, each species feeds in a slightly different way. For example, the Striated Thornbill (opposite), the Brown Thornbill and the Buff-rumped Thornbill are all birds of dry eucalypt forests but the Striated takes its food from the outer leaves of mature trees, sometimes hovering briefly, while the Brown tends to forage in the understorey. The Buff-rumped Thornbill feeds on the ground and in the lower foliage and bark of gum trees.

Other thornbills feed in different habitats. In woodlands the Yellow Thornbill forages in the canopy and in still more open country the Yellow-rumped Thornbill gleans from the ground. The Tasmanian Thornbill is endemic to the State's rainforests and wet eucalypt forests. Learning these differences is helpful and so, too, is learning their different calls and markings. But just knowing a thornbill from a pardalote, fairy-wren or Silvereye (pages 76, 78 and 80) is challenging enough for the novice birdwatcher.

Thornbills move around the bush during most of the year in small parties or flocks, very often in the company of other birds, such as treecreepers, robins (page 84) and pardalotes. The mixed flock affords some protection from predators, and alarm calls from any one member sees the whole group dashing for cover.

In spring or early summer thornbills break away from their feeding parties to build dome-shaped nests woven from bark strips and grass and bound with spider webs. Depending on the species, these may be high in the outer foliage of gum trees, stuffed into hollows or fenceposts, knitted into low vegetation or suspended from twigs or leaves. A well-rounded hole in the front of the dome serves as an entrance and the interior is lined with soft material.

Gardeners able to provide dense vegetation may hope to entertain at least one species of thornbill and maybe even provide a suitable nesting site. In the south-east, Striated Thornbills will set up home in gardens with thick plantings of gum trees and native shrubs. These replicate their natural habitats of gum forests with a well-developed under-storey, and will yield rich insect pickings. Brown Thornbills will venture into the leafier and denser gardens of Canberra and Melbourne. In some towns and farms Yellow-rumped Thornbills forage on lawns and in paddocks, often taking grass seeds. In all cases, there must be dense cover to provide refuges against predators, such as currawongs, hawks and cats.

Robins

Flame: 14 cm
Scarlet: 13 cm
Red-capped: 12 cm
Yellow: 16 cm

To see robins, you may need to venture beyond the confines of cities and towns, but they still can be found in the wilder parts of large city parks, reserves and bushland.

Australian robins are not, as you might expect, related to the robin red-breast of European Christmas cards, despite their similar body shape and size, the same dark eyes and bill, and their quiet and shy demeanour. These Australian birds were called robins by early settlers because they looked and behaved like the bird of their homeland, and the name has stuck. In fact, the Australian robins evolved on this continent tens of millions of years ago. There are 16 Australian species. All are insectivorous and catch their food by watching and pouncing from shoulder-high perches onto the ground, but each has evolved a slightly different lifestyle to avoid direct competition with one another.

Learning to recognise robin species takes time. The buffs and greys of female birds present a conundrum for even experienced birdwatchers but the bright breast colours of some males are helpful. Of the red-breasted robins with black and white wings and backs, the Flame Robin, a common resident of the high country, is the only one with red extending to its throat and belly. The rather dumpier and more distinctly pied Scarlet Robin occupies the woodlands and open forest of both the south-west and south-east. The Red-capped Robin speaks for itself.

Within their range the Yellow Robins—one for the west, and one for the east—are common. They are easily recognised as both sexes have yellow breasts. In the east, Yellow Robins (opposite) live in the stillness of the wet eucalypt forests and rainforests of the Great Dividing Range. Their call, a repetitive 'peep-peep-peep-peep', rings out through the forest. In the west, a similar call can be heard in woodlands and shrublands. If you think you hear a Yellow Robin, stop and wait for a while; you may be rewarded by the silent appearance of a grey back, yellow breast and a pair of dark shiny eyes.

Robins' distinctive nests are usually built in the spouts or forks of trees, but sometimes just on horizontal branches. These substantial, well-formed cups are fashioned from shredded bark and grass, bound with spider webs and often camouflaged on the outside by moss or lichen. Remaining hidden is important to these small birds. Many of Australia's robins appear to be in serious decline, along with other forest and woodlands birds. Surveys and research clearly show that habitat destruction, especially logging, is at least in part responsible.

Eastern
Western

Yellow Robins

Sunbird

10–12 cm

Scarcely bigger than a small child's hand and one of the most delightful birds of Queensland's tropical coastal regions and islands is the Yellow-bellied or Olive-backed Sunbird. Both names describe it well and once the brilliant flash of yellow has caught your eye, you should have little difficulty identifying it. If in doubt, look for the long, sharp, thin bill, shaped like a curved darning needle. The male is distinguished by a chin and breast plate of iridescent blue–black that becomes especially shiny during the breeding season.

Similar in shape to the American hummingbirds, Australia's sunbird displays the same spellbinding feat of hovering on the spot by beating its little wings super-fast while sucking up nectar from flowering trees and shrubs through a long, hollow, straw-like tongue. At other times, it feeds hanging by its strong little legs from vegetation. Spiders, too, form an essential part of its diet and these are plentiful among the tangled multi-layered understorey that festoons tropical creeks and mangroves—favourite haunts of sunbirds.

It's possible that the sunbird's nest may attract your attention before the bird itself but only if you know what you are looking for. Sticky spider webs hold together a sort of vertical hammock of woven bark, twigs and leaves with a side entrance towards the top. In Australia, the construction is unusual, but this bird is only one of a large group of nest weavers that are widespread across the tropical regions of the world.

In recent years, perhaps as a result of rainforest-edge development, sunbirds have increasingly been taking up residency in gardens. They have cleverly adopted handy man-made structures, such as clothes lines and eaves of houses, from which to hang their nests.

Rainbow Bee-eater

up to 28 cm,
counting the central
tail feathers

Do they really eat bees? Yes, they do. They catch them in mid-air around the waist in their long slender bill, well away from their face where they could do harm. They then carry the bee to a perch, knock it senseless and rub the sting out of its abdomen, before swallowing it whole. A bird can consume a hundred bees in a single day. Beneath favourite perches and roosts you may find the regurgitated remains of countless insects.

This beautiful little bee-eater lives in northern Australia throughout the year, but many of them migrate to the south (except Tasmania) in summer to breed. Those that remain in the north will breed either just before or just after the wet season. Bee-eaters favour open country with perches from which to prospect for large flying insects such as bees, wasps, moths, damselflies and dragonflies. Once spied, the bee-eater takes off in hot pursuit. Its pointy wings and two long, slender centrally-placed tail feathers (in adults) give it exceptional mobility in the air. When hawking, it can twist and turn in a split second.

Bee-eaters are smart. Much to the consternation of bee-keepers, many have learnt that a perch near the flightpath of a hive is a top spot for catching dinner. In some instances commercial bee-keepers have retaliated by shooting birds but it is unlikely that the toll these birds take on commercial hives outweighs the benefits they bestow on farmers by ridding them of locusts and other pests.

Most of the time bee-eaters are sociable and can be seen lined up along fencing wire or on branches overhanging watercourses when feeding but, come the breeding season, birds pair off. Males offer food gifts to their mate, and couples vibrate their tails and raise the feathers on their crowns in mutual admiration.

Bee-eaters nest in burrows, which they excavate themselves. Soft, workable soil is an important consideration when choosing a site. Riverbanks, paddocks and golf courses with sandy or loamy soil may be suitable. The female undertakes most of the work. She must dig an almost horizontal tunnel, maybe a metre long, with a chamber at the end. She does this by tipping her body forward onto the 'wrists' of her wing bones while peddling madly away at the soil with her feet and claws. If she needs to break up some clods, she uses her bill as a pick-axe. The hole must fit the bird's body snugly for there are many ground predators to fear, including lizards, snakes, feral dogs and cats and foxes. Both parents rear the young, often with help from other non-breeding bee-eaters.

At summer's end, Rainbow Bee-eaters gather along telegraph wires, sometimes in hundreds, ready to migrate north. They travel at night and some venture beyond Australia's borders, winging their way over the Arafura Sea to New Guinea and even beyond.

Spinebills

16 cm

Here is a bush bird that you should welcome into your garden. It is a small, relatively shy honeyeater that takes nectar from plants often shunned by bigger, more aggressive honeyeaters. Its long curved bill gives it the advantage of being able to reach down into the trumpets and bugles of long-petalled flowers, such as heaths (*Epacris* species) and Mountain Devils (*Lambertia formosa*).

It can also do something that very few Australian birds can do. It can flap its wings at such a rate that it can feed while still airborne. Using its tail as a rudder it can move from flower to flower, dipping its bill into the throats of flowers in much the same way as a hummingbird does. Of course, it has more weight to carry and the wings don't beat as rapidly so it cannot sustain this hovering activity for a prolonged period. Luckily it has strong legs and feet, too, which it uses to cling onto branches and reach into flowers. It has no trouble hanging upside down or balancing on vertical twigs.

There are two Australian spinebill species. The Eastern Spinebill is to be found in woodlands and heathlands of eastern and south-eastern Australia, including Tasmania. The Western Spinebill inhabits similar habitat but in the south-western corner of the continent. Males of both species are handsomely coloured and, although their markings are similar, they are subtly different. In both cases, the females are duller.

If you want to entice spinebills into your garden you will need to grow native plants with the right kind of flowers. Big grevilleas and bottlebrushes will be appropriated by Noisy Miners (page 98) and wattlebirds (page 62). Small-flowering grevilleas, however, may not be considered worth bothering with by the big birds but if spinebills find them, they will certainly feed from them. Try kangaroo paws and miniature banksias, too, and in Western Australia, dryandras.

In the bush, spinebills are territorial about their food plants and often you will notice a small group calling incessantly as they flit from one bush to another. The territorial cry is a high-pitched repetitive 'peep-peep-peep' and it lets other birds know that these bushes are taken. Like most honeyeaters, spinebills eat insects, too. These provide them with the protein they need to stay healthy.

Many native gardeners consider the spinebill to be a challenge to bring into their garden. We know that small birds are declining and spinebills may be one of the first to venture into a well-planted garden. Once these feel safe, you might hope to attract fairy-wrens, thornbills and pardalotes, too.

Western
Eastern

Honeyeaters

At the last count there were 67 species of honeyeaters in Australia and many of them are featured separately in this book. All have a special tongue, a sort of absorbent paintbrush affair that can reach deep into the throats of native flowers such as eucalypts, banksias, grevilleas and bottlebrushes to lap up nectar at high speed. The honeyeaters are equally valuable to the plants as pollinators.

Honeyeaters are the quintessential Australian bush bird. When the Australian continent was breaking away from the supercontinent Gondwana 40 million years ago, the ancestors of today's honeyeaters were on board; so, too, were the ancestors of the archetypal Australian plant family, the Proteaceae. Originating in the closed rainforests of those wetter times, today's members of this family are represented by the banksias, dryandras, hakeas and waratahs, groups that have adapted to the drying conditions. Evolving alongside them have been their key to dispersal—their pollinators, the honeyeaters.

The eucalypts came later. Their family, the Myrtaceae, was present in the Gondwanan rainforests but more as lillypilly-like plants. Eucalypt pollen only appears in the fossil record 34 million years ago. However, their nectar-rich cups, advertised by prominent stamens, enticed the honeyeaters and so the two spread across the Australian continent.

While nectar is the number one food source for most honeyeaters, it certainly isn't for all, or indeed for any, all the time. Nectar is a carbohydrate and provides birds with energy, but all birds, especially growing ones, need some protein. So honeyeaters often eat insects, too, and they feed them to their young. For honeyeaters of the rainforest, fruit is a major component in their diet.

Many honeyeaters move around the continent to take advantage of flowering seasons. Desert honeyeaters, for example, are highly mobile and travel around in feeding flocks. Others, such as the Yellow-faced Honeyeater, undertake annual north–south migrations. Scarlet Honeyeaters, too, move annually up and down the north coast of New South Wales and southern Queensland.

Some honeyeaters venture into our cities and towns. One of the most commonly seen in south-eastern Australia and Tasmania is the New Holland Honeyeater (opposite). Like so many of its kind, this bird is highly territorial and chases away others that seek to muscle in on its feeding grounds.

Another relatively common visitor to leafy suburbs of Sydney and Melbourne is the White-plumed Honeyeater. The Brown Honeyeater, a common resident of watercourses in much of northern Australia, visits gardens in Queensland, Perth and Darwin.

The Blue-faced Honeyeater comes into gardens in parts of New South Wales and Queensland. The Singing Honeyeater is common in Adelaide and Perth gardens and the White-cheeked Honeyeater inhabits Perth suburbs. The distinctive Yellow-throated Honeyeater, one of three honeyeaters endemic to Tasmania, is also a garden visitor.

Figbird

28–30 cm

This bird's common name is fitting, for it is indeed exceedingly fond of figs. Fortunately Australia is well endowed with native fig trees, and the exotic ones often grown by people of Mediterranean descent are an added bonus. So, too, are the native figs we often plant to provide shade in our parks and large urban spaces and it is here that you are most likely to see your first figbirds.

Actually you are most likely to hear them before you see them. As they move around the foliage, they form a noisy mob, their voices a concoction of sharp, clear whistles, musical two-note 'tchok...chair' calls and other see-sawing tunes. They also mimic the calls of other birds, including those of rainbow lorikeets and galahs.

If you think you can hear these sounds and are passing beneath a fig with squishy fruits underfoot, chances are you'll find the figbird up in the canopy picking off the fruits. And if you find one, you'll find others because these birds are very sociable. Since fruits are their staple diet and fruiting trees are not always easy to find, they have learnt to share. When a tree is in fruit in the rainforest it is a bonanza for all the fruit-eating birds, and the figbirds, like others, converge upon it to eat their fill.

Figbirds also visit wet eucalypt forests, mangroves and even woodlands bordering rivers, providing there is suitable food available. Orchards and gardens may offer other fruity attractions. Given their food preferences, it is not surprising that figbirds are described as nomadic; they are always on the move in pursuit of freshly fruiting trees.

Male and female figbirds have quite different plumage. The males (opposite) are likely to catch your eye first, and it's their eyes you'll probably notice first, too, because the red patch of skin around the eyes is their most striking feature, set, as is it is, against a black head. The body is an olive green and the breast may range from green in the south to yellow in more tropical regions. The female (inset) is a discreet brown, heavily streaked on the breast, and with grey–blue, rather than red, skin around the eye.

Indian Myna

23–25 cm

This bird has developed such a fearless association with humans that it thinks nothing of strutting nonchalantly through a busy petrol station or supermarket car park. Here is a bird that has learned to avail itself of food as much from humans as from nature. It investigates the contents of dropped wrappers, polystyrene containers and unfinished snacks tossed into bins with the same detailed attention that it snaps up its traditional fare of insects.

Many believe that Indian Mynas are on the march...down the highways. It is true that they use roads to move between centres of habitation. The air currents created by passing traffic disturb insects on the grassy verges and helpfully flush them out for the Mynas to peck up. Mynas are intelligent birds and they have long been using their ingenuity to get a feed.

Traditionally birds of tropical Asia, they often piggyback on grazing cattle, buffalo, deer and the once-common rhinoceros. They pay for their rides by freeing these beasts from biting insects. Sometimes they hop around the large grazing head, quick to snap up fleeing insects in the wake of blowing nostrils.

Mynas nest in holes and so represent a threat to many hollow-nesting native birds but they don't penetrate far into bushland. They prefer to hop or stride along our city pavements, showing off their yellow legs with matching bills and face patches. Their soft matt plumage is a mixture of dark and milk chocolate with splashes of white on the wings and under the tail.

If you compare them closely with Noisy Miners (page 98) you will see that they look quite different. While both are about the same size and sport yellow legs, bills and eye patches, the Indian Myna is a dumpier, more upright bird and the rather solid colouring of its brown plumage has an altogether sleeker appearance than that of the greyish Noisy Miner. Admittedly both are common birds of the eastern seaboard and their names are confusingly similar but they are spelt differently and these differences reflect the differences in their genealogy. Miners are honeyeaters but Mynas belong to the starling family. Listen to that loud litany of chattering, screaming and scolding and perhaps you can recognise in the flexibility of its voice how it is that the Indian Myna can mimic other birds and even, to a degree, 'talk'.

Noisy Miner

25–28 cm

Not much happens in the Noisy Miner community that everybody doesn't get to know about. If ever a bird was able to attract your attention, it would have to be a Noisy Miner, or more precisely, a mob of Noisy Miners. When these birds get together to defend their territory, they make such a hullaballoo that they could raise a sleeping giant from his slumber.

Although Noisy Miners are actually native honeyeaters, they mainly feed on insects. They are most at home around areas that have been cleared but still retain some trees and other bushes on which to perch and from which to glean. This preference explains why so many of them take up residence in our parks and suburban gardens.

Noisy Miners live in colonies. They keep in touch with one another with several different calls. When another bird, or perhaps a cat or goanna, has the temerity to intrude, or possibly just blunder, into their territory, one loud piping alarm note, repeated incessantly, is enough to alert the entire colony to its presence. Within seconds the whole clan has been summoned and the fight is on. The intruder is shrieked and screamed at and sometimes dive-bombed until it has the good sense to move on. The collective assault mustered by Noisy Miners enables them to take on far larger intruders than they could singlehandedly. Kookaburras, boobooks, goannas, crows and even dogs are all possible targets.

Noisy Miners act collectively, too, when it comes to nesting. If food is plentiful and conditions are good, a colony may raise many broods over a year. A single female builds the nest and incubates the eggs but the whole clan will undertake the duties of protecting the young from predators and bringing food to the nest.

These mobsters are often responsible for excluding the smaller, shyer birds from our gardens but they are fascinating birds to watch. They are also efficient pest-controllers for organic gardeners. Each day this noisy squadron will scour your garden for plant suckers, caterpillars, loopers, psyllids and small grasshoppers.

Bellbird

19 cm

Tinnitus is an infection of the eardrum that afflicts many people. It manifests itself as a constant noise in the ears and appears to arise from exposure to continuous loud sounds; soldiers accustomed to constant gunfire and rock-and-roll musicians are especially prone to tinnitus. When you hear the collective territorial 'ting, ting, ting' of tens of Bellbirds—more properly known as Bell Miners—you might wonder why human inhabitants of these birds' forests do not fall victim to the disease.

The high metallic calls resonate through tall wet forests like hundreds of bells ringing in your ears. So concentrated is the sound that you half expect your ears to pop out of your head. Hearing them is one thing; seeing them another. Their grey–green bodies blend in perfectly with the gum leaves they inhabit. This is a case where a pair of binoculars and a strong flexible neck are usually required.

Bellbirds are honeyeaters and, like all honeyeaters, they have brush-tipped tongues for soaking up nectar. While they do feed on nectar, the mainstay of their diet is a tiny insect that builds itself a sugary shelter on the underside of leaves. This insect is called a psyllid and its covering, a lerp. On the underside of gum leaves in the wet eucalypt forests of the Great Dividing Range these little creatures proliferate and this is what the bellbirds are singing about.

Gathered into colonies of up to 200 birds, their ringing calls are a warning to other birds to stay away. The message is: this is Bellbird country, trespassers will be expelled. And being big won't help. Kookaburras and currawongs are evicted with the same territorial gang violence that they serve out to smaller birds. The only daytime residents permitted to stay are those confining themselves to the dense shrub-level understorey which appears to be a necessary part of Bellbird forests.

Psyllids make their living by sucking fluids out of leaves. Infestations can damage trees significantly. Bellbirds appear to farm the psyllids, culling large numbers for food but leaving enough to keep reproduction, or production, self-sustaining. In this way Bellbirds maintain a constant supply of their food and are able to defend a single territory for many years without having to move on.

Starling

20–21 cm

Despite the beautiful spangle of purple and green iridescence of this adult bird's black body, and despite its commonness throughout eastern Australia, the presence of Starlings—often in huge numbers—seems to go unnoticed.

In fact Starlings are the most widespread birds in the world and in 1850 some bright spark decided to import them into Melbourne where they made themselves at home. They spread throughout Victoria and into neighbouring New South Wales and South Australia. In 1880 another bright spark introduced them into Hobart and now they are comfortably ensconced in Tasmania as well. The intention behind these introductions was that the starlings would act as good pest-controllers, gobbling up the caterpillars and other insects that infested farmers' crops. But, as so often happens with these deliberate introductions, they have themselves become a problem for humans.

Starlings move around in foraging flocks for protection and they feed in open spaces, rooting down into soft surfaces. You may see them on playing fields, golf courses or mud-flats but the cut stubble of rural Australia probably offers them the best pickings. It's true that they will voraciously eat out an area but insects form only part of their diet. Their taste for fruit and seeds invokes the wrath of grape-growers and orchardists, and puts them on the long list of culprits responsible for spreading weeds.

Also of concern are their nesting habits. Starlings nest in holes. Around humans, holes in buildings and walls are practical but near woodlands and forests they occupy tree holes, depriving native birds of their traditional nesting sites. They will even evict existing nesters. They can raise up to seven youngsters in a brood and nest two or three times in a season. No surprise then that Starling populations have been exploding. Determined to keep these birds at bay, Western Australian and Northern Territorian authorities employ shooters to destroy every individual that makes it over their State line.

Starlings travel in black clouds of sometimes hundreds of birds. It is fascinating to watch the 'cloud' changing shape, stretching out and sweeping back on itself, as if it were a single amorphous animal. How do they fly so close together and not bump into each other? At roosting time the 'cloud' descends upon trees large enough to accommodate their collective mass. Jockeying for the best possie, they squabble and screech. So high pitched are some of their notes that they are beyond our range of hearing.

Blackbird

The gardens and parks of temperate Australia are rich feeding grounds for Blackbirds. They love a well-nourished lawn from which they can extract worms. They also appreciate a vegetable patch from which they can pluck the juicy caterpillars of the introduced cabbage moth. (The hairy native cup moths are less appealing.) A good leaf litter or mulch is another rich seam of food. Blackbirds will spend hours tossing this stuff around to unearth the numerous tiny invertebrates sheltering between its moist, dark layers.

When animals are in short supply, gardens usually contain a few plants yielding either berries or soft fruit, both of which Blackbirds love. As if this wasn't enough, clipped hedges and shrubs provide dense bushy nesting sites affording protection from predators and the harsh elements. Is it any wonder then that these birds should become common residents of our backyards?

A conventional garden, with its open area of lawn and edging of shrubs, is also architecturally perfectly suited to a Blackbird's needs. While they are ground-feeding birds, able to bounce their way across a small lawn in 20 hops, they also need perches nearby where they can hide when danger lurks. Of course, in many gardens the number one predator is the domestic cat.

Blackbirds were introduced into Australia from England by homesick settlers who longed for the melodious fluting birdsong of their homeland. Today they are common in the cooler parts of the continent. They have spread north and west but appear to be restricted by humidity on the one hand and aridity on the other. They have penetrated some way into bushland but, with the enticement of well-kept gardens and parks, the bush holds rather less to offer and rather more to fear.

It is easy to tell the male from the female Blackbird. The male is handsomely decked out in jet black plumage and sports a bright yellow bill with matching eye-ring. The female is brown, speckled on her underside. Her quiet colouring underscores her role as chief nest-maker and incubator. He, on the other hand, fiercely defends territory with chasings and clipped harsh alarm notes. He is also a songster of great virtuosity and is often to be heard first thing in the morning and last thing at night.

Australian Raven

52 cm

The Australian Raven is a big black crow-like bird with a raucous grating 'aarwk' call that trails off into a sad descending wail. This is an important distinguishing feature as there are five members of this family, the corvids, and they are all big glossy black birds with pale eyes. In appearance, only the ruffled feathers beneath the chin set the Australian Raven apart from other crows in Australia.

With beaks like tempered steel and superb eyesight, not much that moves and is small enough escapes this bird's attention. As well as insects and reptiles, ravens will take seeds, eggs and baby birds from nests. It is not unusual to see the slow-flying raven, its 'fingers' spread out against the sky, being pursued by a squadron of smaller birds shooing it off their patch.

Ravens are also scavengers and can easily locate rotting carcasses on our roads and in the bush with their remarkably good sense of smell. Once birds of the wild, they are making in-roads into our suburbs, or is that we are making in-roads into their wilderness? Whichever, ravens are now not above investigating a food wrapper or a polystrene cup.

The crow family has a reputation for being highly intelligent. Certainly some individuals have no problem hiding food for a day and remembering where they've left it. Australian Ravens are known to perform a cunning trick: working together they are capable of separating a weakened lamb from its mother and the herd, pecking at its tail until it falters and drops. Once felled, the lamb has little chance.

Australian Ravens are long lived and bond for life. They have generally benefited from land clearances and pastoral activities but they need tall trees in which to build their large nest of twigs. These are usually jammed into the fork of a branch, which provides a brace in high winds. The nest is lined with bark, wool or hair and the female lays up to four eggs. She undertakes the incubating and babysitting duties while her mate must keep the whole family plied with food.

In Tasmania and southern Victoria you are more likely to see the Forest Raven and in northern and central Australia the Torresian Crow is a common resident. The nomadic Little Crow occupies some of the driest habitat in central and western Australia. The Little Raven, which is only very slightly smaller than the Australian Raven, is also nomadic but only within south-eastern Australia; in the high country, large flocks of them gather each year to feed on bogong moths. Determining differences between these species requires a really practised eye.

Koel

39–46 cm

Finding the female Koel is even harder than locating the male. However, I include Koels here because the clear, high-pitched call of the male rings across many Australian cities during the warmer months and it is easy to recognise: a two-note 'coo-ee' that rises a step at a time to a feverish pitch before culminating in a series of trumpeting screeches. The call is repeated again and again in the male's unstinting effort to attract the almost silent (at this stage) female.

Each year Koels arrive in northern and eastern Australia over spring and early summer from South-east Asia and New Guinea. They remain hidden in the dense canopy of trees but the male's calls are a sure give-away. By late September the first birds have reached Brisbane and by the beginning of October they are in Sydney.

At about the same time the Dollarbirds (page 114) and Channel-billed Cuckoos (page 112) arrive from the north, too, so keep an eye out for these harbingers of summer. All three birds are noisy, big and confident, and you may notice how their presence causes considerable anxiety among the local bird populations, most of which are in the midst of their nesting season.

If you follow the cries of the male Koel you will eventually locate high up in the canopy of a tree a large black bird with a long tail and a bright red eye. This is one time when a pair of binoculars is invaluable. Having found your black bird, the red eye will confirm that it is a Koel. Koel trees are as likely to be in parks and gardens as they are in forests or woodlands.

Koels are cuckoos and, like all cuckoos, they lay their eggs in the nests of other birds. The female's lovely, subtle plumage—a patterning of dark brown and white bars and blotches—distinguishes her from the male and affords her the camouflage she needs to skulk into the nest of a host bird to deposit her eggs (inset). Red Wattlebirds, currawongs, Magpies and friarbirds all serve as unwitting hosts to Koels' eggs. These poor host parents become rushed off their feet catering to the hungry offspring of the much larger Koels.

Once independent of their foster parents, the young birds roam the neighbourhood, learning to feed themselves. You can tell the young from the adult Koels by their brown, rather than red, eyes. At this time males fall relatively silent but the loud insistent cries of the adult females start up. It has been observed that mother Koels reconnect with their young once they are fledged. The bonds are sealed by endless squawkings around the neighbourhood morning and evening for weeks on end. Towards the end of summer, however, the Koels depart for the north, young in tow. Other visitors leave around then, too, and the bush returns to the more familiar sound of native birds.

Spangled Drongo

28–33 cm

Perhaps it is the elegantly flipped-up tips of its mermaid-like tail or the gorgeous sleekness of its blue–black iridescent body that suggests that the Spangled Drongo must be a bird of tropical persuasion. Indeed, these birds are common in northern Australia and still further north than that. Some birds are sedentary but many from New Guinea and northern Queensland leave after winter and migrate further south to breed and here they often visit botanic parks and private gardens.

You may be lucky enough to see one as far south as Wollongong or Jervis Bay in New South Wales, but this would be a rare event indeed. Still, they are not hard to see, given their preference for tall, bare-leaved look-out branches and their loud rasping calls and tearing cries, which will alert you to something unusual. Although not particularly large, the male Spangled Drongo is a striking bird. Its black coat shimmers in the sunlight with a blue metallic lustre on the wings and a spangly blue on the head and body. Its eyes are bright red and its silhouette is unique. The female is similar but slightly smaller, and young birds are a sooty black, yet to acquire their sheen.

Drongos are very active aerial hawkers that like to hunt at the edges of rainforests and mangroves where a sunny break in a closed canopy provides good lighting and an enticement to flying insects. From their look-out perch they sally out in pursuit of often fast and erratic prey. Undaunted, drongos can respond with acrobatic twists and turns and only occasionally are they out-paced. Having snapped up prey in a slightly hooked bill, birds return to their perch to consume a well-earned snack. Drongos also use their bill to winkle out grubs and spiders from beneath bark and to tear away rotten wood, termite mounds and the channels of burrowing larvae. Fruit and nectar supplement their diet.

Spangled Drongos often move around in mixed flocks of relatively big birds and may take up a high look-out position while flock members forage for food. In the event of a predator entering the arena around the feeding birds, the Drongo sentinel utters a sharp alarm call to warn the busy birds gobbling away in the bushes. It doesn't do this out of the kindness of its heart. A flock of birds working the bushes for food flushes out many flying insects, which the Drongo may snatch in mid-flight before returning to its perch.

Drongos construct their nests high up in the canopy on the outer branches of densely foliaged trees. They lash the twining stems of vines to horizontally forked branches and weave a shallow bowl of tendrils, grasses and spider webs. Their dark colouring, the cover of foliage and their blotchy eggs serve well as camouflage. Both parents will sit on the eggs, tend the young and defend the territory aggressively against intruders.

Channel-billed Cuckoo Up to 65 cm

The first time you see a Channel-billed Cuckoo, it's a bit of a shock. You don't expect to see a cuckoo the size of a small eagle but that's how big it is. The heavy-duty bill, however, is a sure sign that this ain't no eagle.

Most people hear the Channel-bill before they see it. If you're familiar with the cries of the Koel (page 108) you may at first think you are listening to a male Koel with a sore throat. The Channel-bill's call is louder, less tuneful and grating. Channel-bills often croak as they fly. If you think you hear one, look up and you may have the good fortune to see this large, awkward-looking bird...sometimes a pair. The body size, bill shape and raucous cry should leave little room for doubt.

The Channel-billed Cuckoo is a summertime visitor to Australia. Its arrival heralds the warm weather. Some people have dubbed it the Rain Bird, presumably because in the north it heralds the Wet. Like all cuckoos, it parasitises the nests of local birds, laying its own eggs there and leaving the unwitting parents to incubate them and feed their young. There are stories of deception that imply great cunning: while the male Channel-bill distracts an already-nesting bird, the female sneaks round the back, evicts the existing eggs from the nest and pops a quick one of her own in. Australian birds known to 'host' this anti-social behaviour are the Torresian Crow, Collared Sparrowhawk, Australian Raven (page 106), Pied Currawong (page 172) and Magpie (page 170).

With no parental duties to tie them down, visiting birds are free to feast. You can set your clock by the Channel-bills' journey each day from their roosts to their feeding grounds. They feed on figs, and with many of our parks and gardens dotted with old majestic figs of mammoth size, it is no wonder that Channel-bills are becoming more common visitors to our cities and towns.

There is probably another reason, too, why they are coming so close. Currawongs, one of their favourite hosts, are also becoming more common in urban areas. With good food and obliging currawongs playing surrogate parents, Australia is looking like a prime breeding destination for the Channel-billed Cuckoo in the future.

Dollarbird

About 30 cm

Dollarbirds fly over the skies of India, China, Korea and Japan but those that visit Australia usually come from southern Asia and New Guinea. These summer migrants to northern and eastern Australia come here to breed and to escape the oppressive heat of the tropics. Like the Channel-billed Cuckoo (page 112) and the Koel (page 108), their arrival in Brisbane and Sydney heralds the start of summer.

These dumpy little birds belong to a family known as rollers, so named for their habit of rolling and tumbling in flight. They are skilled aeronautical fliers, specialists in the art of capturing fast- and sometimes erratic-flying insects, and even small birds. In tune with the activity of their prey, Dollarbirds mostly confine their hunting exploits to morning and evening sessions.

To perform to their optimum, Dollarbirds need high perches bordering wide-open spaces. It is hardly surprising then that these are birds of forest edges. They select the highest perch they can find with unobstructed aerial views. These may be old bare branches jutting out into the sky and it is often as a silhouette that these birds are first seen. Telegraph wires have some merits as good lookouts but they rarely exceed tall trees in height.

From these high places, Dollarbirds launch themselves to pursue their prey. Watch them as they fly. Surprisingly swift, their ability to change direction in a split second is remarkable. They fan out their tail feathers to provide an effective rudder and tilt it appropriately to alter course. They can also tilt their entire body at almost 90° to one side or the other. In so doing they reduce drag and so escalate their speed. It is during these tilting exercises that you may catch the glint of iridescent blue–green as the sun's rays fall upon their upper wings.

Dollarbirds are usually first noticed because of their voice, a sort of loud grumbling and cackling chatter, often uttered while in flight. It takes a bit of attention to track the birds down and get a good look at them. A pair of binoculars will reveal a curious-looking bird with unusual colouring: a brown head, blue breast, bright red legs and bill, and a greenish blue body and wings that sometimes flash in the light. The underside of each wing sports a white crescent. It is this marking that in some person's mind was reminiscent of an American dollar coin and has given rise to the bird's common name.

Swallows

Welcome: 15 cm
Barn: 16 cm
Red-rumped: 18 cm
White-backed: 14 cm

Probably the first time you saw a swallow it was perched high up on a telegraph wire, or perhaps on a bare branch overhanging a creek or river, very likely in the company of a string of fellow swallows. In fact these little birds spend most of their lives on the wing, so it is worth learning to recognise their silhouette against the sky.

Swallows hawk for flying insects, often quite high in the sky. To meet the challenges of the speedy and erratic flight of many winged insects, swallows have developed strongly forked tails and pointy wings. Also useful is the swallow's wide gape and some stiff bristles clustered around the base of its bill, which expand the area over which prey can be caught. Not only do swallows feed on the wing, they also drink this way, skimming the surface of lakes and rivers.

Three swallow species inhabit Australia. A fourth, the Red-rumped Swallow, occasionally visits the north. Most common is the pretty Welcome Swallow (opposite), with a distinctive chestnut face and bib, an iridescent blue–black back, and dark wings, tail and head. It mostly inhabits southern and eastern Australia, with occasional sightings in the Top End. Tasmanian populations depart to the warmer mainland during winter.

The Barn Swallow looks very similar. Only the blue–black collar under its chestnut chin and the whiter underparts easily distinguish it. It visits northern Australia each summer, probably from Asia, and a few flocks trickle southwards down both coasts. This is the same species that flies each summer from Africa to Europe and North America to breed.

Most swallows build mud nests. They painstakingly gather hundreds, maybe thousands of beakfuls of wet mud which they sculpt into a cup-shaped nest and line with soft materials such as grass, wool, hair or feathers. We often see swallows darting under bridges, porches, eaves and cliff overhangs. These sheltered spots make ideal nesting sites.

The White-backed Swallow inhabits dry, open country and ventures inland where there are few aerial structures in which to build nests. Perhaps this is why these birds excavate a tunnel in sand or loose soil to serve as a roost and nest.

Swallows are easily mistaken for martins or swifts. It is possible to see all three of these aerial insect-catchers hawking simultaneously on a warm, insect-infested early morning or evening. Check their silhouettes. Swallows have deeply forked tails, the two outer feathers trailing almost like streamers. Tails of the slightly smaller martins are almost squared off in flight. The unrelated swifts are mostly larger than both, with broad, sickle-shaped wings. Swifts fly at dizzy heights and are, as their name suggest, the swiftest of them all.

Welcome Swallow

Black-faced Cuckoo-shrike

30–36 cm

This elegant, slender bird of considerable size has a distinguished appearance. The black face mask studded with shiny black eyes contrasts with its sleek two-tone silky grey body. You will usually see it sitting up on a telegraph wire or the look-out branch of a tall tree. Watch it fly and identification is assured. Its seemingly relaxed, almost slow, wingbeats result in a distinctive undulating flight pattern. Most distinctive of all is the way in which this bird shuffles its wings on alighting upon its next perch, causing some people to call this bird a Shufflewing.

The Black-faced Cuckoo-shrike is neither a cuckoo, nor a shrike. Rather it belongs to a big family of about 70 species which live throughout Africa, Asia, New Guinea and Australia. Of the seven species inhabiting Australia, the Black-faced Cuckoo-shrike is the most widespread and common.

Mostly this bird depends on insects and other creepy-crawlies for food. It has a number of hunting strategies. Sometimes it pursues and catches prey in mid-air. Other times it watches from a perch and pounces on prey on the ground. Its most unrefined, though clearly effective, ploy is to crash into the outer leaves of trees with its wings spread wide in a bid to net whatever there is to eat within its circumference. Because of its powerful beak, it can take on relatively large prey, which it may savagely bash senseless before consuming. To supplement this protein-based diet it also takes fruit and seeds.

Being a tree-dweller, it is found in most wooded areas, except rainforest. In dry parts of the interior it makes do with whatever shrubby vegetation it can find. Seemingly unfazed by the large-scale, noisy activity of humans, it has come into our cities and towns where parks and gardens yield year-round pickings.

It nests in trees, building a stout, shallow saucer of twigs and shredded bark bound securely with spider webs. Both parents feed the young until they are able to fly. After breeding, some birds may form flocks and migrate to suitable winter grounds; others remain, moving around a wide area to fulfil their dietary needs.

Muttonbird

41–43 cm

Have you ever come across a bedraggled bird corpse swept up on a beach? Chances are it's a Muttonbird. This bird is indeed common but it spends most of its life out at sea, fishing. The corpses we see are weak and exhausted birds that have been swept off course by storms at sea.

Seabirds do it hard. The ocean is an unpredictable and dangerous place. The extraordinary annual migration marathon of the Muttonbird is excessively demanding and fraught with danger. Following the summer breeding season along the Bass Strait and in Tasmania, tens of millions of Muttonbirds head east to sea. Before reaching New Zealand, they change direction and take a northerly route across the Equator, passing east of Japan's many islands to loop around the edges of the Pacific Ocean. They spend the Northern Hemisphere's summer fishing in the Bering Sea, around the Aleutian Islands and in the Gulf of Alaska, before heading south in late September, passing offshore of Washington and California, into the central Pacific and back home to breed.

Many landbirds will nest in the first year of their life, but Muttonbirds do not begin breeding for at least five years. For them survival is such a tough game that it takes that long to become reliable and competent parents; in their case this means weathering the elements and bringing home the fish.

Muttonbirds are also known as a Short-tailed Shearwaters. All shearwaters fish for a living. Their legs are set well back on their undercarriage. As with the engine on a boat, this is the best place for propulsion through water but it does mean Muttonbirds flounder about hopelessly on land. It's no coincidence that their nests—metre-long burrows in sand mounds beneath tussocks of grass—are located high up on vegetated sand-dunes or cliffs into which they can almost directly fly and from which they can drop down into the air.

If you get a chance to visit a Muttonbird colony, rug up and go at dusk. As night falls you will just be able to make out in the gloom hundreds of intrepid birds coming into land to roost for the night. This exciting experience puts you in touch with the elements and gives you just a taste of what it might be like to live constantly at the mercy of the sea.

120

Wood Duck

44–55 cm

Wood Ducks don't look like typical ducks, nor do they behave much like ducks. They look more like small geese and they're just as happy to perch in trees as sit on open water. While they are prepared to get their feet wet, how many do you see up-ending in true dabbling-duck style? None. Of course, not all ducks up-end, reaching down into the mud to pull up the bulbs of aquatic plants, like Australia's Pacific Black Duck (page124) or the introduced Mallard (page 126). Some dive for dinner and others, like the Wood Duck, graze on the shoots, roots and seeds of plants growing in soaks and along the edges of water. And that is why you see Wood Ducks so often on golf courses and playing fields, and on small farm dams.

They do, of course, swim, especially when they are vulnerable on land, such as during moulting or when they are with young ducklings. At such times they will skim just beneath the water's surface, sieving out small aquatic animals and weeds in their bill.

Wood Ducks, like so many of Australia's native birds, nest in tree hollows. These may be very high above the ground. For fledglings raised in these skyscrapers, the first venture out of the hollow is undoubtedly a very scary event. They simply drop out of the hole and fall to the ground below. Their still-fluffy plumage allows them to float rather than drop like a stone, giving them some 'brakes' in the air. Nevertheless, it must be a rude awakening to life out of the nest. And often the trial is not over. Nesting trees may be as far as a kilometre away from water. In such cases parents escort their brood on the long trek. The journey may be treacherous, with many beady eyes watching hungrily for a straggler.

Another name for this species is the Maned Duck. This refers to the male's small crest of feathers along the back of his head. It's easy to tell males from females. His crest and whole head is chocolate brown and his back and wings a sleek plumage of dark brown and pale grey. The female's colouring is more subdued, but the white strip above and below her eye is distinctive.

Throughout most of Australia, Wood Ducks are common and widespread, but in the Top End, where competition between ducks is fierce, this duck is an unusual sight. Overall, however, these birds have taken advantage of the human preoccupation for digging holes and filling them up with water, and their numbers are on the rise.

Pacific Black Duck

48–61 cm

This is Australia's most common and familiar duck. Wherever there are lakes, dams and quiet creeks with floating or emergent aquatic weeds, this duck shouldn't be far away. It spends much of its life on water, feeding on invertebrates, seeds and weeds. In shallow water it 'ducks' down to shift through the soft sediments, keeping itself up-ended for up to a minute by paddling madly with its feet. Its characteristic short quacks are synonymous with still waterways.

Shallow bodies of water may dry out during droughts, so most ducks are highly mobile. Black Ducks are no exception, but when conditions are good, these ducks will raise up to 10 chicks in either a grassy ground nest or a tree hollow lined with down.

Ever since the importation of Mallards into Australia, the Black Duck has been in danger of genetically engineering itself out of existence. While female Black Ducks will not succumb to the advances of pure-bred male Mallards, the same cannot be said of female Mallards to those of male Black Ducks. These two will happily mate and produce offspring crosses. The female Black Ducks then become quite prepared to take on hybridised males and so the pure-bred Pacific Black Duck's genetic pool is being constantly diminished. Now Australia (and New Zealand) are populated by hybridised ducks and it is only too easy for a birdwatcher to get confused.

Recognising a male Mallard is easy (page 126). Distinguishing a pure-bred female Mallard from a female pure-bred Pacific Black Duck is much harder: the Black Duck is generally a darker brown but the give-away is in the finely arched black face-markings of the Black Duck. When it comes to the hybrids, it gets really tricky. Look at the legs and feet. Those of Mallards are orange, while those of the Black Duck are dull green or brown. Check the bill. In the male Mallards it is yellow and in the female Mallards, pinky brown. The Black Duck's bill is a bluish grey. Lastly, Mallards have a patch of iridescent blue in their upper wing which, in the Black Duck, is closer to green.

Confused? You'll soon get your eye in. If you see a brown dabbling duck with dark eyebrows and orange feet, you're probably looking at a hybrid Mallard/Pacific Black Duck.

Mallard

52–67 cm

Whenever I look at a Mallard drake (male) I am reminded of the British World War II saying about Americans, 'they're oversexed and they're over here'. Aside from the grumblings of British men about the apparent sexual prowess of the allied Americans, it is true that Mallards are introduced birds with a prodigious taste for our native population of ducks and this has resulted in some considerable confusion on the part of us birdwatchers. They are especially fond of Pacific Black Ducks (page 124). About their size and shape, they either can't tell the difference or don't care.

It cannot be denied that the male Mallard is a handsome chap. His iridescent green head, set off by a bright yellow bill and a narrow neckband of white, is his most striking feature. The female is quite different; a softer-looking, brown and white speckledy creature. Her only concession to strong colours is a small panel of purplish blue in her wings, a feature she shares with the male.

It is not always easy to tell female Mallards (top) from female Black Ducks. The wing panel, although more greenish than bluish in the Black Duck, can be misleading given its iridescent sheen, but an important clue is the colour of the feet and legs, which in Mallards are orange. Another telltale feature is the distinctive white underwings of Black Ducks, which are absent in Mallards.

The Mallard's propensity for breeding with other ducks is not confined to Australian Black Ducks. Many domestic ducks have a good genetic measure of Mallard in their make-up, too, and there is no denying that as a species they have been extremely successful.

Mallards are now widespread throughout the world. In America and Europe they migrate south in cold weather but in Australia they are mostly sedentary, preferring the comfortable lakes of city and town parks and gardens. It was to decorate such places, and as game, that these ducks were introduced from England in the 1860s. Perhaps their reluctance to venture into the bush is a blessing. At least Australia's more mobile Black Ducks can escape geographically, if not genetically, from the attention of randy Mallards.

Dusky Moorhen

About 38 cm

Dusky Moorhens belong to a group of birds sometimes known as the gallinules. 'Gallina' is Latin for small hen and describes the group well. Other Australian members of this group are the Tasmanian Native-hen, which occurs only in that State, and the Black-tailed Native-hen, a native of inland waterways. Gallinules also bear some resemblance to the Purple Swamphen (page 132) and have the same habit of flicking up their tail to display their white patches as a warning.

In size and overall appearance Dusky Moorhens look rather like Coots (page 130) but their face shield and bill are red. They are also shyer birds. They stick to the dense cover of the reeds, sedges and water weeds that grow at the margins of water bodies, including quiet creeks. They are less sociable, too, and hang out only in ones, twos or, at most, small groups. Coots and Moorhens have similar tastes in food but Dusky Moorhens prefer not to get their heads too wet, so up-ending or diving like Coots is out of the question. Instead, they pluck, pick and pull at vegetation and glean from the surface of the water or just beneath it. They will also forage on damp ground, picking up seed or moisture-loving invertebrates in their bill. Their large, spreading feet provide balance and prevent them from sinking when they are moving through sodden beds of down-trodden plants or squelchy sediments.

Dusky Moorhens have an altogether nervous disposition. They are easily alarmed and make a quick dash for cover with a loud 'kruk' at the slightest disturbance. Sometimes they will take to the air briefly, their greenish legs trailing behind, and relocate themselves away from the perceived threat. When paddling, they tend to jerk their head back and forth and flick up their tail, the white patches presumably intended to frighten off predators.

Clutches of up to 10 eggs hatch into a large, bowl-shaped nest of reeds, sedges and grasses tucked into growing beds of aquatic vegetation or sometimes perched on a knobbly emergent root or log. The chicks develop their characteristic yellow-tipped red bill while they are still downy.

Moorhens are doing nicely in Australia but they cannot make a go of things without good cover. The massive curtains of cover provided by the introduced willow trees that now line many of our quieter waterways are no doubt a great boon to them.

128

Coot

About 38 cm

Sometimes this wetland bird is called a Bald Coot, presumably because of its white face shield extending from the white bill. Sometimes people confuse this bird with the Dusky Moorhen (page 128), another inhabitant of wetlands. They are more or less the same size but the face shield and bill of the Dusky Moorhen are red with a yellow tip and its eye is dark. The Coot has reddish brown eyes.

Coots are one of the few swimming birds that can be found on deep permanent water-bodies, such as artificial reservoirs and dams. Except when breeding, they prefer open water. In winter, they may cluster together to form dense rafts. Being strongly territorial, they will defend their feeding grounds with vigour.

Coots are mostly vegetarian. They like the tender shoots of water plants, but they also take aquatic larvae, worms, surface-dwelling insects and small fish. To reach all the food available they will up-end and dive. The wobbly fleshy lobes on their feet help them swim, up-end and paddle around: on the downstroke of the feet, the lobes are spread to give surface area to the forward thrust, while on the upstroke they collapse along the sides of the feet to reduce resistance to the water.

In flood years, breeding activity increases. As the breeding time approaches, Coots retreat to the edges of the water. Both the male and female gather weeds, sedges and reeds which they mound up into a raised platform to form a floating nest. To prevent the nest from floating out into open, unprotected waters, it remains tethered to standing vegetation. The female lays up to 12 eggs and the parents take turns on the nest. The young birds develop a reddish face shield and bill. With so many to feed and an uneven hatching regime, the parents are careful to treat their brood even-handedly. A voracious, greedy chick may get a severe reprimand in the form of a shake and dunk and perhaps suddenly find itself parted from its family and in the precarious situation of having to look after itself. Many predators have Coot on the menu!

Unlike some other wetland birds, Coots have adapted well to the spectacular hydrological engineering feats of humans. They have a worldwide distribution that stretches from most of Europe in the west, across China, South-eastern Asia, Japan and New Guinea to Australia, and more recently New Zealand.

Purple Swamphen

44–48 cm

The Purple Swamphen is quite common around the large ornamental lakes of parks and golf courses in towns and cities. A quite bulky, gangly-looking bird, its small head, massive feet and almost chicken-like body give it an awkward shape. But with its red legs, eyes, bill and forehead shield, you should have little difficulty identifying it.

Tame birds are easy enough to see. In fact, they can be quite cheeky, approaching picnickers for a free hand-out. But Swamphens belong to the rail family, a group of characteristically wary or shy birds that spend most of their time skulking around reedbeds at the edges of swamps and marshlands. In the wild, Swamphens are no different. They emerge from thickets of reeds only during the early morning and late afternoon when the necessity to find food drives them out into more open spaces. However, sometimes curiosity gets the better of them, and they will come out to inspect anything new in their territory, including uninvited humans. Unless useful, the bird usually departs giving the intruder 'the flick'.

The flick is a flash of white rump, visible only when the tail is raised. It seems to signify 'go away, choof off' but it may mean far more as this signal is frequently given both on land and when swimming.

Swamphens are not keen swimmers and rather feeble fliers but their extraordinarily large feet are well adapted to keeping them afloat while they are trampling through reedbeds or mud. Their long legs allow them to run quite fast and will take them into deep water without them having to swim.

The strong legs and feet are often used to pin down prey, such as frogs or snails. Sometimes they will attack small ducklings and they have a reputation for stealing eggs. But their more usual fare is the shoots and fleshy roots of reeds, sedges and grasses, which they tug up from the gluggy bottom with their feet and bills. They also use their legs to construct their nests, trampling and bending down reeds and dragging them into mounds and platforms for nesting, roosting and feeding.

Black Swan

About 100–140 cm

Australia's Black Swan is unmistakable. There are few differences between the sexes but males are slightly larger, with slightly longer necks.

Swans live on large expanses of fresh or brackish water where there is plenty of room for take-off into the air. Much of these water bodies must also be shallow, no deeper than a metre or so, so that the swans can reach down with their long necks to reach submerged food. For swans, and indeed most waterfowl, water-storage dams are a barren wasteland.

Swans are vegetarians. The only animals they consume are incidental. They will graze at the water's edge or in flooded swamps and paddocks. They dabble at the water's surface for floating pondweed and algae, and up-end to reach the bulbs, tubers and roots of reeds and sedges. If feeding in brackish water, they regularly seek out fresh water to drink.

An adult swan has a mighty load to lift off the water and into the air. In order to fly it must treat the surface of the water as an airstrip, powering its lift-off with the flap of its massive wings, while rapidly running with its webbed feet. Once airborne, it tucks its legs up into its undercarriage to reduce drag and its wings stretch out to a span of two metres.

Birds have a couple of invaluable adaptations to lightness and flight. First, their bones are not dense like those of mammals; they are honeycombed with air, making them much lighter. Second, birds have extra internal air bags; these reduce weight and assist in supplying oxygen for the energetic business of flying.

And what goes up must come down. The swan descends onto the water still flapping its broad wings quite fast. If it beats too slow, it will plummet like a stone from the sky. Preparing to land, it splays out its webbed feet in front of it and, with downturned open wings still flapping, water skis along the water's surface until it can stop and sit down.

Black Swans move around a lot in search of fresh feeding grounds and suitable breeding sites. They visit lakes, billabongs and flooded swamps. Often they fly at dusk, dawn or night, travelling in small parties, flying in V formation and bugling or honking as they go.

Swans are believed to mate for life. Couples nest on islands or in dense reedbeds, pulling together a conglomeration of twigs, algae, water weeds and sedges. Into this the female lays 4–10 eggs. Incubation duty is shared. As one comes to relieve the other, the pair greet one another with much neck stretching, wing opening and bugling. In just over a month the young are hatched and, decked out in their grey downy feathers, they immediately take to the water.

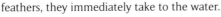

Cormorants

Great: 70–90 cm
Pied: 65–80 cm
Little Black: 60–65 cm
Little Pied: 50–60 cm
Black-faced: 60–70 cm

Wherever there's water, you'll find cormorants. They inhabit coasts, estuaries, rivers and inland water systems everywhere. Fossils of ancient cormorants have been found in central Australia dating back 20 million years to a time when the centre was indeed wet. Today it is rarely so but when the floodwaters do come to central Australia, cormorants still flock from the continent's edges to converge on the wetlands to breed.

Cormorants eat mostly fish, along with molluscs, crustaceans and other aquatic animals. They dive for their food, holding their wings close to their sides underwater, and paddling with their webbed feet, which are set well back on their body. They swim swiftly, their body and neck stretched out sleekly, pursuing darting prey. The hook on the end of their bill forms an invaluable weapon for dispatching slippery items. Cormorants have been recorded trailing in the wake of foraging platypuses and harvesting small aquatic organisms disturbed from the ooze by these busy little monotremes.

Cormorants often perch on rocky outcrops or on branches above a flowing river, holding their wings out to dry like so much washing in the wind. Unlike those of many birds, cormorant feathers are not waterproof: they get soaked when fishing, so to keep them in good working order, the birds must regularly take time out to dry them.

Cormorants will breed at any time of year provided food is plentiful. Most cormorants nest either in trees and shrubs above water or on offshore islands, often in colonies. These can be crowded, noisy places where males perform courtship displays on the nest of twigs they have gathered to entice females to partner up with them. They throw back their head and quiver from side to side while croaking raucously. The nest is sometimes lined with seaweed or reeds and will hold up to five eggs.

Of the five species in Australia, two are almost entirely black except for their yellow bill. The largest, the Great Cormorant, lives in many parts of the world and, in accordance with its size, is attracted to large bodies of water. The Little Black Cormorant is distinctly smaller. The three other species are black and white. Only when the Pied stands beside the Little Pied (opposite) can they be easily distinguished. The Little Pied tends, however, to inhabit smaller bodies of water, such as farm dams.

The fifth species, the Black-faced Cormorant, sometimes known as the Black-faced Shag or Great Black-faced Cormorant, lives almost entirely at sea and is found only along Australia's southern coast and around Tasmania.

All cormorants

Australasian Gannet   85–95 cm

When looking out to sea, have you ever seen a large bird dropping out of the sky into the ocean like a falling star? Look again. Is it white with a gigantic pointed bill that pierces the water's surface like a dart? Does it fold its wings back towards its body as it plunges seaward? You have just identified one of the world's most proficient seabirds, the gannet.

Gannets may be confused with terns (page 140), but these are smaller fishers with a more slender shape and wingspans greatly in excess of their body length . In more tropical seas, you are likely to come across the gannet's relatives, the boobies, but throughout the more temperate oceans around Australia the gannet reigns supreme.

A young gannet will spend nearly its entire life at sea, even sleeping on water. Fish provide all its dietary needs and it is superbly adapted for their capture. It hunts alone or in flocks. When alone it may target a single large fish; flocks are more likely to target shoals. In a split second a gannet can drop out of the sky from as high as 30 metres. A network of airbags just beneath the surface of its skin absorbs the impact of these dramatic changes in air pressure. The bird doesn't dive directly onto the fish, but rather below it, taking the fish from beneath. Its upper mandible is sharply serrated and the fish is swallowed underwater. Within 10 seconds, it's all over and the gannet is once more airborne.

Life at sea is hard and there is a lot to learn. Development is relatively slow compared with land-dwelling birds. It may be a couple of years before young gannets acquire their sleek white adult plumage with trailing black wing feathers and a wash of pale yellow on the head. They may not commence breeding until they are seven years old. But once they do reach sexual maturity, they may spend up to half the year at the breeding colony.

Australasian Gannets breed in crowded colonies on precipitous cliff-faces and other rocky outcrops of offshore islands. Their nests are little more than a depression in the ground, perhaps with some earth and seaweed cemented together with guano (bird poo). There is no more than pecking distance around each nesting pair. The egg—usually one—is incubated by the parents' webbed feet, which are well supplied with a network of warm blood.

The pair swop incubator–fisher roles regularly. On the return of the fishing partner they perform elaborate greeting rituals. Standing opposite one another on tippy toes, with their wings slightly open and and their chests lightly touching, they stretch their necks up and raise their bills in the air, then waggle them about, softly fencing with them.

Egg laying commences in October. By April or May the fully-fledged young have left the colony. Many of them will travel long distances. On the unpredictable and sometimes wild ocean winds, they will hone their flying and hunting skills until they, too, are ready to become parents.

Terns

Crested: 44–48 cm
Caspian: 53cm
Sooty: 42–46 cm
Fairy and Little: 22–26 cm

Distinguishing between a tern and a seagull (page 142) is a major turning point for the learning birdwatcher. Both are usually white with black and grey markings. Their legs and bills may be yellow or red, as well as dark. Both, too, are commonly seen fishing just off the coast or standing around on rocky promontories or spits of sand in estuaries or at the beach. Often groups of terns and seagulls gather together on one bit of land although, if you look carefully, you will notice that there is some segregation between the groups and not much interaction. The clues lie in the body, bill and wing shape and in how the two groups fish.

The bodies of terns are torpedo-shaped and their wings are long and narrow with a distinct 'elbow'. The body is often shorter than the span of a single wing and the tail is usually forked. Terns have long, pointed bills. The whole body architecture is designed to fold into a dart-like shape that can plunge into the sea on target.

The bodies of gulls, on the other hand, are dumpier and the wings are broader. Gulls do sometimes plunge awkwardly into the sea but they are more accomplished at fishing in flocks on schools of fish and at scavenging on land along the tideline. Not surprising, then, that gulls' legs are long and capable of rapid motion on land, while those of the more ocean-going terns are short and less useful on land.

Many of the terns hardly visit the mainland at all but, of the 20 or so species seen around the Australian continent, 14 are known to breed in our waters. With the exception of the Whiskered Tern, which inhabits inland fresh waters, terns have evolved to life on the wing and the rigours of the sea. Some, including the Sooty Tern, may not even set foot on land or water for literally years. When they eventually nest, it is on offshore islands well away from the hurly burly.

Terns are notoriously hard to recognise at the species level. Perhaps one of the most common and easiest to identify is the Crested Tern (opposite). For Australia's second largest tern (after the giant, red-billed Caspian Tern), every day is a bad hair day. With spiky tufts sticking out at the nape from its black crown and a bright yellow bill, it is distinctive.

The Little Tern and the Fairy Tern are both small and have black crowns and yellow legs and bills. They enjoy the sheltered sandy islets that often eventuate where rivers and creeks drain into the sea, and it is here that they nest. These birds are very vulnerable to disturbance from human traffic, dogs and four-wheel drive vehicles. If you see some small terns gathered on a sandy spit, give them a break and take a wide berth around them.

Crested Tern

Silver Gull

41 cm

Whether you live inland or beside the coast, this bird should be familiar. Silver Gulls are the best known, most ubiquitous and widespread gulls in Australia. They are easy to tell apart from other gulls.

Adults have dashing red legs, bills and eye-rings that contrast strongly with their pale grey back and wings, and the white head, breast and belly. The wing tips are black with white 'windows'. Among the flock you may see other similar-looking birds with black legs, bills and eyes, and mottled brown plumage. These are juveniles that have yet to acquire their adult colours.

There are a few other gulls that visit our coasts in summer, all of them smaller than the Silver Gull, but none are as common as our large black-backed Pacific Gull which inhabits the coasts around Tasmania and the southern mainland. This impressive gull with a chunky yellow bill tipped with red may come under competitive pressure from the similar-looking Kelp Gull, which has recently established itself in the same habitat.

Because Silver Gulls are so common, they give us an opportunity to watch them closely. Their body language is diverse and complex and their behaviour provides some insight into the behaviour of birds in general. Indeed gulls were the subject of some of the first scientific studies into bird behaviour undertaken by the Nobel Prize-winning Dutch zoologist, Nico Tinbergen. Watch them for expressions of aggression, submission, begging, flirting, greeting and rage. The range of communication may surprise you.

The population of Silver Gulls in recent years has exploded. Their success is built, almost literally, on our rubbish. These birds take any opportunity to get a feed and they eat almost everything. Beside hawking, fishing and stealing eggs, they have learnt to glean from the activities of humans. They follow boats for food tossed overboard and the plough for unearthed insects. They gather for handouts from fishermen and seaside picnickers, and they frequent sewage outfalls and municipal dumps as bulldozers stir up human garbage. Given their propensity for birds' eggs, they are threatening the ability of some endangered birds to reproduce. This is just one of many instances where human activity has an unseen, indirect impact on the lives of other species.

Silver Gulls may have taken advantage of the man-made environment big time but they still remain tied to the sea for food and to remote landscapes for nesting sites. They nest in colonies on offshore islands and sandy spits, in marshlands and on floodplains. When the rains come, many Silver Gulls depart from the coast to breed on the islands that poke above the surface of shallow inland lakes. When Lake Eyre filled in the 1970s thousands of Silver Gulls chose this inland site for nesting in preference to coastal ones.

Cattle Egret

48–53 cm

Have you ever looked into a paddock of cattle and noticed white stork-like birds standing around the cows? These are Cattle Egrets. If you get the chance, stop and watch them and you'll soon realise what these birds are up to. Each egret travels in the wake of a grazing cow. As the cow's legs move forward a host of tiny animals living in the grass try to hop, crawl or fly to safety to avoid being crushed to death. Quick as a flash the egret stabs at these creatures with its sharp dagger-like bill and down its slender throat they go.

Although Cattle Egrets feed in paddocks, they roost and nest in trees overhanging swamps or billabongs, often paperbarks. You can tell quite a bit about a Cattle Egret by looking at it. If it's pure white with a bright yellow bill, it's a non-breeding bird. If it's pure white with a black bill, it's a young bird yet to attain its colourful bill. If the white plumage is adorned with buff feathers on the head, breast and back (opposite), it's a breeding bird. During courtship the yellow bill turns red except for the tip.

In northern Australia, breeding is during the Wet. In southern Australia, it begins in spring and goes through summer. Based on the principle that there is safety in numbers, they nest in colonies, in bushes or trees. They look awkward standing up on branches on their long legs and there is a lot of flapping about to find suitable landing pads and keep their balance. As so often with colonial nests, jostling for a good possie involves much honking, grunting and clacking. Somehow each couple manages to build a flimsy platform of sticks. From egg laying onwards the colony is likely to receive the unwelcome attentions of a host of potential predators: kites, eagles, falcons, currawongs and goannas by day; owls and rats by night. The eggs and nestlings of inattentive parents more engrossed in bickering than attending to their duties become vulnerable to attack.

The Cattle Egret is one of five egrets in Australia. The other four are all very fond of fish and stalk them in the shallows of freshwater lakes, mangroves and reefs. There are tales of these aquatic egrets rounding up fish with other fishers such as cormorants, herons and pelicans. It seems egrets associate easily with other animals to benefit themselves.

The Cattle Egret was originally a bird of Africa and Asia. It has expanded its range into Europe, America and, in the 1930s or 40s, Australia. Given its habits, it is not surprising that it only arrived in Australia after bushland areas began giving way to farmland. That said, they do feed themselves unassisted in wild areas, such as the Coorong of South Australia, so they are not entirely dependent on grazing beasts.

144

Herons

Nankeen: about 58 cm
Striated: 45–50 cm
Pied: 43–52 cm
Great-billed: to 110 cm
White-necked: 75–105 cm
White-faced: 66–69 cm

Herons like to hunt alone for obvious reasons. If you make your living stalking prey through water, the last thing you need is a bunch of mates literally muddying the waters and scaring away the food. So if you spot a lone long-legged, long-necked skinny-looking bird standing in a watery landscape, chances are you're looking at a heron.

Herons are built for a life of spearfishing: their long legs, short tail, superbly flexible long neck, brilliant eyesight and dagger-sharp bill equip them for stealth and lightning strikes. Patient and still, they watch the ground or water for any movement with intense concentration. Their quarry may be a fish, a rodent, an insect, a worm, a snake, a crab or even a little bird. It is not unusual to see a heron or two in wet pasture or on playing fields after heavy rain, waiting for flooded-out animals to make their escape into their hungry mouths. Occasionally a heron will puddle the water around with one foot to flush out any lurking prey in the mud or vegetation. Less often you might see a heron depart from its ice-maiden stance and hot-foot it through the shallows in pursuit of a swift tasty dinner.

The differences between egrets (page 144) and herons are subtle. Typically egrets are white all over. In the breeding season they are festooned with long breeding plumes like bridal veils. Herons bear less showy breeding plumes and generally display some colouring, usually grey or brown, along with white.

Six heron species typically inhabit Australia. The short-necked Nankeen or Night Heron is small and rufous coloured. It skulks about in the shallows of mangroves and other quiet bodies of water. The smaller Striated Heron patrols northern and eastern coasts and mangroves. The little Pied Heron lives among northern wetlands and tidal estuaries. The heavily built and dark-coloured Great-billed Heron is the tallest of Australia's herons and the only one unique to the continent. It, too, is a heron of the tropics and finds its food at the edges of mangrove-lined channels and along tidal mudflats. Also quite tall is the White-necked Heron, which has a white neck and head but a dark grey back and wings. It is widespread across freshwater floodplains but still nowhere near as common as the White-faced Heron (opposite).

Herons may be solitary hunters but they usually breed in colonies. They build their stick nests up in dead or living trees and raise usually two to four young. In the case of the White-faced Heron this may be quite far from water. The colonies are known as heronries.

White-faced Heron

Ibis

Sacred: 68–75 cm
Straw-necked: 60–76 cm
Glossy: 48–61 cm

The hunched body shape and long curved bill of the ibis is familiar to many of us. Unfortunately the Sacred Ibis has become a bit of a fixture in some of our city parks, where it scavenges through litter bins and on the ground for the rubbish we leave behind. Most ibis, however, still live the traditional life of a bird forever fossicking in the ooze for worms, molluscs, crustaceans and insects.

Out in the bush you will see ibis feeding on the edges of floodplains, where young grasslands shelter crickets and caterpillars. If you're observant, you'll notice how active these birds become during wet weather. Flocks fly in from outlying areas to take advantage of flooded pastures. As the rain softens up the ground, making penetration easier for their bills, ground- and grassland-dwellers flee the rising waters and the ibis clean up.

There are three ibis species in Australia. Most widespread is the Straw-necked Ibis. As its name suggests, long straw-coloured plumes that become particularly showy during the breeding season fall from the front of its neck down to a white breast. Its black back and wings glint an iridescent green and russet red in the sunlight. The smaller Glossy Ibis may look completely black but its plumage, too, has a metallic sheen of green and bronze. Neither of these birds particularly cares for the tidal mudflats of more saline waters where they must sometimes seek a meal, but the Sacred or White Ibis (opposite) is a more adaptable species.

Ibis breed in the network of extensive wetlands afforded by the Murray–Darling Basin of New South Wales and Victoria, especially in places like Macquarie Marshes. Another important ibis breeding ground is Lake Alexandrina in South Australia. After good rains these places burst into life and all three ibis species gather in large breeding colonies, often mixed with spoonbills. Curiously, ibis like to roost and nest in trees, usually around water but, where vegetated islands provide adequate protection, they will make their untidy nests of sticks and vegetation on beds of swamp grass, each only a nip away from the neighbours on all sides.

Farmers do not always recognise these birds as friends but ibis are wonderful pest-controllers. Their long, probing bills can dislodge grubs and larvae from holes and crevices, and flocks that descend on young crops in search-and-destroy missions will systematically rid large areas of chomping insects, such as locusts.

All Australian ibis

Spoonbills

Take one look at the bill and there's little doubt what bird this is. About 20 centimetres long, almost flat but very slightly downcurved and serrated along part of its edges, it spreads out like a flat spoon at the end. Spoonbills sweep this highly specialised feeding tool through shallow water, their gape slightly ajar. They move slowly forward, scything from side to side as they go. The end of the bill is sensitive to touch and detects floating, swimming, crawling or drifting organisms. Spoonbills snap up small fish, crustaceans, molluscs, tadpoles, frogs and insects. The serrated edges allow water to escape before prey is swallowed. The bill is ideal for rooting around in the soft sediments for the fleshy bulbs and tubers of water plants. This disturbance of fine mud particles also flushes out small animals. Since eyesight is less important than touch in capturing prey, spoonbills sometimes feed at night when shrimps and fish are easier to catch.

Given their feeding strategies, it is little wonder that spoonbills are exclusively water-birds. In Australia, there are two species. Although they look similar, it is not hard to tell the difference. The Yellow-billed Spoonbill is slightly larger and its bill and legs are yellow, whereas those of the Royal Spoonbill (opposite) are black. In both cases the bill colour extends onto the face as bare skin and particularly striking on the black head of the Royal Spoonbill is a yellow patch above the eyebrow and a red one on the forehead.

It is rare for two such closely related species to share such similar habitats, diets and foraging techniques, yet these two species are often seen happily feeding, flying and even nesting together. There is, however, a subtle, but important, difference. The bill of the Royal Spoonbill is shorter but the 'spoon' is wider and swept through the water faster, allowing it to catch faster-moving fish than the Yellow-billed Spoonbill, which spends more time probing into the sediments to yield 'slow' food: yabbies, insect larvae and water bugs. So these two species do not directly compete and may even assist each other.

Spoonbills breed in trees or lower dense vegetation near water, often in the company of ibis. Unlike ibis colonies, which are full of loud quarrelsome birds, spoonbill colonies are quieter, more sedate places and behaviour at the nest is more restrained and delicate.

Spoonbills develop distinct breeding plumes. Royal Spoonbills sprout elegant white plumes from the nape of their neck, while Yellow-billed Spoonbills develop buff plumes on the upper breast and fine black plumes on their tail.

In the mucky places inhabited by these birds, good hygiene is essential and spoonbills spend a lot of time preening; where the bill cannot reach, the feet do the work. Even at the nest, parents preen their fluffy white chicks and so instil the practice from an early age. Royal Spoonbills especially always look immaculate.

All Australian
spoonbills

Brolga

100–140 cm
Females smaller

The elegant Brolga is Australia's only native crane. It is a common bird around the billabongs and shallow freshwater floodplains of the country's north, but rarer in the south.

Brolgas are tied to water by their diet. Sedately patrolling the edges of billabongs and swamps they prod the oozy bottoms with their long, sharp bill for the roots of water plants, particularly the rhizomes of their favourite food, bulkuru sedges. They also take small aquatic creepy-crawlies and, given the chance, frogs and snakes, too.

In northern Australia Brolga populations gather together or disperse according to conditions. In the Wet, they spread out into the inland plains to avail themselves of young shoots and freshly hatched animals. As they fatten up and food becomes plentiful for their young, breeding commences.

Brolgas usually pair for life. Together they construct the nest, which may be on dry ground or shallow water. Nests on dry ground are barely more than a roughly pull-together platform of twigs and grasses, but those built on water are large mounds of reeds and sedges dragged up from surrounding beds of vegetation or flown in from nearby. Both incubate the eggs—usually two. Within a day or two the young leave the nest but it will take them several weeks before they become proficient flyers.

As the Dry approaches, the shallow waters recede and evaporate through the hot days. Brolgas must fly to more permanent waterholes. They travel in large flocks, their necks outstretched, their long dark grey legs trailing behind, trumpeting loudly to one another as they go. The broad wings, with their dark tips splayed out like fingers, beat slowly and deeply, providing them with considerable lift and power.

As billabongs and swamps continue to dry out and they must compete for the shrinking supply of water creatures and plants, the Brolgas congregate in ever-increasing numbers. In the south of their range they depend almost entirely upon man-made bores and dams.

Brolgas are given to dancing. This impressive spectacle is performed by all the world's cranes. They dance in pairs, bowing, flapping, pointing their bills skywards, advancing, retreating, springing up into the air, then landing as lightly as a bubble. As one pair breaks out into dance, the surrounding group and sometimes the whole flock become infected with the same exuberance.

Since 1966, Brolgas have had to compete with a newcomer on the mainland: Sarus Cranes. Probably originating from South-east Asia, they were first spotted in Queensland and are now found sporadically throughout the Top End. Of similar size and appearance, they can be distinguished by the red, rather than dark grey, legs and the more extensive patch of bare red skin on the head.

Jabiru

130 cm high

The more correct common name is Black-necked Stork, for it does indeed belong to the the worldwide family of storks, but the name Jabiru sounds more compelling to me.

Seeing a Jabiru for the first time is a truly thrilling experience. There is something primordial about this bird. For a split second you may wonder if you've just stepped back in time to a lost world. On recovery from this disorientating experience you should look more carefully. What makes it so different? Is it the sheer size? The long thin red legs? How is it so different from that other long-legged beauty of the Top End, the Brolga? Sure, the black and white body plumage is different and the Brolga's legs are dark brown or grey. Yes, the body is a little deeper but what really sets it apart is the massive black bill and the continuity of that blackness onto the domed head, extending all the way down the long neck until it meets the shoulders. In the sunlight the sleek head and neck shimmer with a metallic purple and green iridescence.

This is certainly a bird you will want to see—the perfect excuse for a holiday up north. Although we can never hope to see it in the southernmost parts of Australia, I include it here among the 'common' birds of Australia because, for residents of the Top End, sooner or later, this is a bird they can surely hope to tick off their list of 'must sees'.

One look at this stork's immense bill tells you that it is built for catching fish, and not just small ones. It will also take frogs, crabs, snakes and turtles; all are eaten whole. Nor is it above feeding on carrion—foraging for food can be an exhausting business. Intense concentration is required to catch prey slithering, jumping and swimming through the reflective water and slippery mud and vegetation. At times the Jabiru will chase quickly after elusive prey, its wings held aloft, perhaps to create shadow or to intimidate an animal so it freezes stiff with fright. Long limbs require rest, and when not hunting the Jabiru hunches down, tucking its neck into its shoulders and letting its heavy bill drop downwards.

If food is plentiful, Jabirus will nest at any time of year. Both sexes build a huge nest of twigs and vegetation in a tree or bush above or beside water. You can distinguish the female only by her yellow iris (opposite); juvenile birds are brown.

A Jabiru in flight is an impressive sight. The neck is extended (unlike a heron's), the red legs stretched out behind and the theatrical black-and-white underwing markings are fully displayed. The powerful deliberate strokes of the broad wings can lift this stork surprisingly far aloft and it travels considerable distances on the warm thermals so prevalent in the north.

154

Oystercatchers

Pied: 48–51 cm
Sooty: 49–41 cm

While strolling along a lonely beach you might have the good fortune to see one or more oystercatchers. They are quite shy birds, so approach them quietly. They are extremely wary, especially when nesting, and will take to the air with high-pitched peeping alarm calls at the slightest disturbance.

The body shape of an oystercatcher is quite recognisable but if you're in any doubt, look for the long, straight bright red bill with matching legs and eye-ring. Two species live around our coastlines but you shouldn't have any difficulty telling them apart. Their names give away their distinctive plumage; the Pied (opposite) has a dapper livery of black and white, while the Sooty is entirely black.

The stout, steel-like shaft of the oystercatcher's bill is not just an adornment. It is an invaluable tool for smashing and prising open shellfish and for prodding down into wet sand to extract burrowing marine worms and crustaceans. Oystercatchers love to eat the tender bodies of animals in shells. Shells may serve as heavy-duty armour against many potential predators but against the relentless prying of the oystercatcher's bill, crabs, mussels, limpets, marine snails and pipis are helpless. Their only defence is to hide.

Oystercatchers are usually seen in pairs or with this year's young. Occasionally, where food is plentiful, feeding flocks, especially of Sooty Oystercatchers, may gather. More often a pair patrol a strip of coastline and guard it from fellow oystercatchers. Sooties generally prefer rocky shores and reefs, while Pieds are better adapted to life on sandy beaches.

These different habitats apply to their nesting locations, too. Both do little more than gather some coastal vegetation into a shallow scrape between boulders or in sand dunes. The Sooties may gather some shells and pebbles around as well. The two to three blotched brown and white eggs, although well camouflaged, are vulnerable to disturbance by humans and dogs and to predators, such as foxes, dingoes and goannas. Pied Oystercatchers are becoming rare on some popular beaches, so always tread with care and keep dogs on the leash.

All oystercatchers

Little Penguin

33–40 cm

Australia's Little Penguin may seem like a rather dumpy awkward bird on land, but in the water it's another story. Its short, fat body becomes a streamlined torpedo shape, perfectly formed for swimming and diving. Its little legs and webbed feet, good for only waddling on land, transform into a rudder, while its wings, incapable of flight, have evolved into flippers that make wonderful propellers in water. Equipped in this way, penguins can dive and swim fast for their dinner of crustaceans, shoals of darting fish and exceedingly swift squid.

Most penguins are inhabitants of Antarctica's freezing sea ice or sub-Antarctic islands, but a few have adopted warmer lands. Of the 17 species existing in the world—all of which live exclusively in the Southern Hemisphere—Australia is fortunate to have its own native penguin.

Little Penguins often stay out at sea fishing for days on end but in the breeding season they return to land in droves each night. There are breeding colonies all around the coast and islands of southern Australia, but the best known, and posssibly the biggest, is on Phillip Island, 60 kilometres south-east of Melbourne. The 'penguin parade' there is certainly worth a visit.

As night falls, rafts of penguins appear in the surf. As they come onto the sandy shore they move as fast as they can up into the dunes. Some of them even fall over in their anxiety to reach their burrows in the sand beneath hummocks of vegetation, rocks or man-made structures.

In mid-winter the female usually lays two eggs in the burrow. For just over a month the pair will take it in turns to incubate them. Once hatched, one parent will remain behind with the chicks for the first three weeks, while the other brings home dinner. Within a further three weeks the young are fledged. Only then can the parents moult. All birds renew their feathers to replace damaged ones but, given the lifestyle of a penguin, heavy wear and tear is inevitable and a regular new sleek plumage is essential for survival.

Australians have a great affection for their only native penguin and they are determined to keep it safe. Volunteers in Tasmania have gone so far as to knit 15 000 penguin jumpers at the request of the Tasmanian Conservation Trust. These are stored in Oil Spill Response Kits around the State for use in the event of an oil spill. Oil that penetrates the inner feathers may harm their insulating and water-proofing properties and recovering penguins eager to preen themselves clean can gum up their bills and may swallow poison. The jumpers will keep the penguins warm and dry and discourage preening until a full recovery is possible.

Australian Pelican

160–180 cm

Have you ever looked up into the sky and seen what might be a small aeroplane...or an ultralight or a gigantic bird? If it's a bird, chances are it's a pelican. With a wingspan of 2.5 metres, these bulky birds are the largest flyers in Australia. Their huge bill and fleshy pouch on the end of a long, retractable neck are unmistakable.

Given their size you might expect pelicans to be poor and clumsy flyers. Even though they can weigh over 6 kilograms, they are in fact highly proficient flyers, because they employ a couple of clever tactics. To keep a heavy bird airborne would usually require a lot of continuous wing flapping, which saps the bird's energy. But with their large, broad wings pelicans can rapidly attain considerable height. They can then catch a thermal, a pillow of air with sufficient density and propulsion of its own to allow the pelican to glide along upon it. Spiralling up on these thermals, they can ride the air currents and glide great distances.

Pelicans are social birds and they sometimes cooperate to catch fish, their staple food. Several swim close together to corral fish tightly; then in unison they dip their heads below the water's surface, filling their cavernous mouths with water and fish. Then, lifting their mouth pouches above the surface, they allow the water to drain out of the sides of their bills, before throwing back their heads to swallow their catch.

Large, permanent bodies of brackish or fresh water may keep some pelicans sedentary but most are nomadic and travel long distances in flocks to find food and good breeding sites. They save energy in the air by each flying directly behind the wing tip of the one in front. The pelican behind can take advantage of the puff of rising high-pressure air left in its wake. That is why you sometimes see pelicans travelling in a V formation.

Pelicans around the edges of the continent have an uncanny way of knowing when torrential downpours are falling in the outback and these irregular and rare events trigger thousands of pelicans to travel inland. In a really wet year, channels of rushing water may run for hundreds of kilometres and spill into the shallow saltpan of Lake Eyre to form an inland sea several metres deep. Fish eggs that have lain dormant for years are flushed out and mass hatchings attract swarms of other waterbirds. The deserts spring to life with fresh vegetation, frogs, snakes, insects and shield shrimps, all released from their time capsules by the rains.

The pelicans take this opportunity to breed. Colonies of up to 15 000 birds have been recorded. If food remains plentiful they may raise a second family, but conditions in the desert can deteriorate rapidly and chicks not yet fully fledged are sometimes abandoned by their parents.

160

Magpie Goose

82–92 cm

The image of hundreds, if not thousands, of pied geese with orange legs and bills flapping their broad wings to lift off from expanses of freshwater swampland is synonymous with Australia's Top End. Southerners make pilgrimages to such places as Kakadu National Park and Fogg Dam in the Northern Territory, Townsville Common, Hasties and Willetts Swamp on the Atherton Tableland, Lakefield National Park on Cape York Peninsula and Lake Kununurra on the Ord River of north-western Australia to see this sight.

This northern distribution has not always been the case. Before 1900 Magpie Geese bred in the lower reaches of many southern rivers in New South Wales and Victoria but they were shot for food and poisoned because they invaded crops, and their wetland habitats were modified by irrigation works. Today you can only see numbers of these birds in the south at Bool Lagoon Game Reserve, south-east of the Coorong in South Australia.

Close up the Magpie Goose looks almost like a cartoon goose. The knob on the top of its head looks like the sort of swelling you might expect from being knocked on the head by a brick. Its eyes have a not-with-it, vacant look. Its orange feet are only partially webbed and set uncharacteristically forward on the body for a goose or duck and its matching bill has a hook at its end. These anatomical features have led some researchers to believe that Magpie Geese evolved before our modern ducks and geese. But such features make perfect sense for life in unpredictable wetlands. When swamplands dry out, being able to walk, rather than swim, to food is an advantage; a hook on the end of the bill makes a good digging tool when baked clods of clay cake nutritious seeds and tubers.

At the onset of the Wet, huge flocks of noisy honking Magpie Geese disperse from the edges of permanent deep lagoons and billabongs that have provided their Dry-season refuge to migrate to the shallower floodwaters of the swollen rivers. They gather in 'camps' at swamp edges, sometimes roosting in paperbark trees. Morning and evening they feed on aquatic grasses or up-end, stretching their long necks down to reach the bulbs of vegetation rooted in the mud. The reeds and spike-rushes, withered by the Dry, put out a new lease of life and provide the geese with both food, shelter and nesting material.

As water levels rise, the density of spike-rush beds increases and the geese are able to trample it down sufficiently to form large mounds of vegetation for their nests, which often float. Ideally, breeding begins at the end of the Wet, when the sedges are at their most dense. The geese nest in colonies, pairs sharing in the incubation and rearing of young. Each year the race is on to raise the chicks before the swamps dry out. Some years end in tragedy, but more often the young birds grow fat and healthy. When water and food become scarce, they accompany their parents back to the permanent waterholes to wait out the Dry.

Masked Lapwing

34–38 cm

You've probably seen these birds, easily identified by the bright yellow 'mask' or wattle of skin that hangs down from either side of the face, in paddocks and on the grass verges of roads, and not given them much thought. Most of the year, they are unassuming birds that go quietly about their business. During the breeding season, however, pets and children should keep well away from nests as reports of dive-bombings are frequent.

A feature of southern Masked Lapwings is a little spur that sticks out from the front of each wing; these birds are sometimes referred to as 'spur-winged plovers' and they do indeed belong to the plover family.

The nests of Masked Lapwings are extremely vulnerable. In open ground the pair scrape a shallow hollow free of vegetation and line it simply with twigs, grass and sometimes dried cow dung. Fields of stubble, paddocks, sandy spits, mudflats, marshes, caravan parks, airstrips and golf courses are all likely sites. The pair dedicate themselves wholly to their parental duties. At no time is the nest left unattended. They take turns to sit on the well-camouflaged eggs, while the other feeds, usually close by in order to keep a watch for possible predators...of which there are many. Some, such as currawongs and foxes, come deliberately for a feed; other nests fall victim to the careless tramplings of stock, four-wheel drives and humans. At the slightest threat, day or night, the sitting bird's high-pitched 'keek-kee-kee-kee' call alerts its partner to return to the defence of the nest. You may have lain awake in your bed and heard this loud, urgent call pierce the night air and wondered what life and death drama is playing itself out beyond the comfort zone of your doona.

There is one clever nesting trick lapwings use to confuse predators. They often act as decoys, appearing to be wounded and therefore tempting prey. They move away from the nest, trailing an apparently broken wing; the predator sees an easy meal and gives chase...away from the vulnerable chicks or eggs. Once the predator is well away from the nest, the perfectly healthy adult can break cover if things get hairy. This decoy strategy to protect young birds is employed by several other species of ground-nesters.

The Banded Lapwing is a similar-looking but smaller species. It lacks the yellow wattle but retains the bright yellow eye-ring and beak. It has a white stripe through its eye. A red wattle just in front of its eye looks, from a distance, like a large, red beauty spot. Similar in behaviour and choice of habitats, its distribution overlaps in many places but it is the lapwing most commonly seen in Western Australia.

Magpie-lark

26–30 cm

You should have no difficulty distinguishing this bird from a Magpie (page 170). It is smaller, has a pale eye and is a very different shape. It is less easy—but more fun—trying to tell the male Magpie-lark from the female.

Both are the same size, shape and colouring but the patterning of black-and-white plumage is subtly different. Look at the face. The female (opposite, bottom) has a white throat, whereas the male's is black, and he sports a pronounced white eyebrow (opposite, top). Just to complicate things, however, juveniles have a mixture of these features: the white throat of the female, though less extensive, and a white eyebrow like the male, but not with the same stylish sweep.

Magpie-larks are known as Peewees or Peewits because of their high-pitched call, two loud clear notes of alarm which ring across the flat lands they inhabit. Males and females also sing duets, holding their wings slightly out from their bodies like opera singers.

You may encounter these birds on golf courses, playing fields or the verges of road-sides. In short grass they can easily find food, mostly insects plucked in their tweezer-like bills, and snails which they skilfully winkle out from their shells. While they appreciate regularly mown grasslands, their natural habitat is wide, open woodlands, particularly the moist borders of inundated land. Also known as mudlarks, these birds are often found patrolling estuaries and the edges of creeks and dams. Here they collect not only food but mud for nest building.

At the beginning of the breeding season both male and female partners undertake endless trips from wet places carrying mud in their beaks sometimes 20 metres up into a tree. Together they construct a bowl-shaped nest which they cement onto a horizontal limb and line with soft grass or feathers.

Magpie-larks are widespread and until recently it was thought they were more or less sedentary. However recent research has shown that there is a marked increase in the Magpie-lark population in the Top End during the winter. It is certainly true that these birds have benefited from human activity, in particular our carefully tended grass-scapes and the digging of dams.

This seemingly mild-mannered bird has a curious habit: it has been known to attack not just glass and hub caps of cars but people's eyes. This is thought to be a case of mistaken identity: the bird, seeing a mirror image of itself in a reflective surface, takes it for an intruder and, in defence of its territory, attacks and collides with an unexpected object.

Butcherbirds

Black: 32–42 cm
Pied: . 32–36 cm
Black-backed: 26–28 cm
Grey: 25–30 cm

Butcherbirds earn their name from their habit of wedging freshly killed prey into the narrow fork of a tree and leaving it to hang in much the same way as a butcher might hang a piece of meat on a hook. If they don't consume it on the spot, they'll return later to feed, tearing it apart with the deadly hook on the top mandible of their bill.

Butcherbirds hunt by stealth. Perched on the lower branch of a tree they watch the ground for movement and pounce on small rodents, reptiles and insects. From trees and bushes they also pluck chicks, eggs and small birds such as sparrows and Silvereyes.

Although butcherbirds are discreet hunters, their voice is loud and distinctive. In fact their lovely rollicking tunes are more recognisable than the birds themselves. Their songs are often remarkably elaborate and young birds stay on after they are fledged to help their parents raise the next year's brood while learning the songs. It is amusing to listen to young birds faltering over difficult phrasing or timing as their music-teacher parents patiently run through a song for the umpteenth time. Family singsongs are a common occurrence once young birds are grown, especially at dawn. Variations in songs are enormous, not just between species and across regions, but even among individuals.

Each butcherbird species has a slightly different patterning of white, black and grey. In some, but not all, the female is smaller. The Pied Butcherbird (opposite) is a sleek-looking species with a dashing black head and breast that meets a white top collar and flank. The wings and tail are pied. Although widespread, it is absent from Tasmania, much of southern New South Wales and Victoria. If there is sufficient tree cover, it is common along roadsides, on farms and in many outer suburbs.

Only on Cape York Peninsula will you find the similar but smaller Black-backed Butcherbird. Its white chin and breast set it apart from its black-chinned and breasted counterpart. The large Black Butcherbird also hunts in the shade of the north's tropical forests and in Darwin ventures into gardens bordering mangroves or paperbark swamps.

Pied
Black
overlap

In Adelaide and Melbourne the widespread Grey Butcherbird hunts in bushy gardens, even in inner suburbs. It generally has a greyer back than the Pied but, as many young birds of both species are grey, it is the distinct white collar curving upwards from a pale breast that best distinguishes it. A completely separate population of Grey Butcherbirds lives in the Top End; some consider these to be a separate species: the Silver-backed Butcherbird.

Grey
Black-backed

Magpie

The sweet carolling song of the Magpie is so synonymous with the bush, and indeed many gardens and open public spaces, that we hardly notice this big black and white bird. And how many of us can tell it from a currawong? Look on page 172 and you will see that there are endless differences, but on first inspection they do look alike.

Magpies prefer areas where the trees meet the short grassy flatlands. Here they can roost safely in the trees and feed on buried grubs and worms in the ground. Remarkably, they can hear the scrapings of feeding larvae underground and this is why you sometimes see a Magpie tilting its head to one side and then the other as if listening...that is exactly what it is doing.

Magpies are common residents of football fields, golf courses, parks and gardens with suitable open and closed spaces. In such places dominant pairs of Magpies establish a territory. Here they may remain throughout their lives, raising families, aerating the lawn with their sturdy bills in search of tasty morsels and declaring their territorial rights. In suburban areas, where food is plentiful, territories are small compared with those in less bountiful bushland or grazing country. Magpies generally live in small family groups. All members of the group defend the family territory from other Magpies by vocal yodelling and chasing away intruders.

Come the breeding season, the dominant female selects a suitable nesting site high in a tree and she alone collects the building materials and constructs the nest, furnishing it with a soft lining as a final touch. Materials may be unconventional, such as fencewire and rope, provided they serve their purpose. Nests are quite large and deep and sometimes smaller birds adopt the basement for their own nests.

The female lays her eggs and incubates alone but her mate attends her regularly with food and keeps a lookout for predators. During the breeding season security in the territory is stepped up and all members will dive-bomb unwelcome visitors, including humans. Each year stories of schoolchildren receiving head wounds from over-zealous parents make the press.

Nesting magpies are fastidious mothers. Once the chicks hatch, the female removes the eggshells, and all the faeces are whisked away before they touch the nest. She continues to brood the naked, blind chicks full-time, but as they acquire down and feathers she will hunt with her mate to feed the family. At four weeks, the fledglings are enticed from the nest by food. Poor flyers and unable to fend for themselves, the next few weeks are critical to their survival. As their skills improve, the parents become increasingly tetchy. Once self-reliant, the young may be banished from the territory, to join roaming bands of feeding magpies. In time they may find a mate and establish their own territory.

Currawongs

Pied 40–50 cm
Grey: 45–53 cm
Black: 46–48 cm

Many people don't know a Pied Currawong from a Magpie. Study their photos in this book carefully (see page 170). Both are black and white, relatively large, and members of the same family but that's where the similarities end.

Pied Currawongs are blacker than Magpies and they have bright yellow eyes; Magpies have brown eyes. Look closely and you'll notice the heavy-duty slightly curved black bill of the currawong. Slightly less intimidating is the Magpie's straight bill which, except in the case of young birds, is mostly white with only a black tip. Another difference is their stance. While Magpies stand more or less upright, currawongs are uncomfortable on the ground and lean forward when perched on branches.

Currawongs are birds of the forest. From high perches, they survey the lay of the land and check out what's for lunch, then swoop down to pluck, among other things, young nestlings from their nests. Their loud, clear cries pierce the air of wooded areas, especially at daybreak and sundown. Songs are varied and elaborate, often sounding like animated conversations. They are also accomplished whistlers.

Pied Currwaongs are widespread across the eastern seaboard. In the drier parts of southern Australia and eastern Tasmania there are also Grey Currawongs. In Tasmania alone, the Black Currawong is a common visitor to highland campsites, moving down to lower, warmer ground in winter. In fact the Black Currawong is not entirely black. It still retains the white tail tip of all currawongs and the white 'windows' in the wings, although these may only be visible in flight; the white undertail coverts of other currawongs is missing, as is the white rump of the Pied.

Currawongs have eclectic tastes. As well as taking eggs and nestlings, they raid orchards for exotic fruits and feed on ornamental berries. Mostly, however, they are voracious carnivores and many of them start breeding just before the summer cicada season, when youngsters can feast on these newly emerging fatty insects. In a shallow nest of sticks high in a tree they may raise two youngsters.

Currawongs travel considerable distances to find food. Pied Currawongs have traditionally summered in the higher country of the Great Dividing Range, migrating down to the coastal plain in the cold winters. Here they often feed on the berries of such garden weeds as privet, camphor laurel, lantana and cotoneaster, the seeds of which they then spread into the bush in their droppings. Recently, however, rich garden pickings have induced them to stay on into the spring nesting season. Their propensity for stealing eggs and young birds may be a contributing factor to the loss of smaller garden birds.

Pied Currawong

172

Useful Information

BOOKS

Attenborough, D., 1998, *The Life of Birds,* BBC Books, London

Barrett, G., Silocks, A., Barry, S., Cunningham, R. and Poulter, R., 2003, *The New Atlas of Australian Birds,* Royal Australasian Ornithologists Union, Melbourne

Debus, S., 2000, *The Birds of Prey of Australia,* Oxford University Press, Melbourne

Flegg, J., 2002, *Photographic Field Guide: Birds of Australia,* 2nd ed., Reed New Holland, Sydney

Ford, H., 1989, *Ecology of Birds: An Australian Perspective,* Surrey Beatty & Sons, Chipping Norton, NSW

Goodfellow, D. & Stott, M., 2001, *Birds of Australia's Top End,* Scrubfowl Press, Darwin

Low, T., 2002, *The New Nature: Winners and Losers in Wild Australia,* Penguin, Melbourne

Morcombe, M., 2000, *Field Guide to Australian Birds,* Steve Parish Publishing, Brisbane

Pizzey, G. & Knight, F., 2003, *Field Guide to the Birds of Australia,* HarperCollins, Sydney

Simpson & Day, 2004, *Field Guide to the Birds of Australia,* 7th ed., Penguin, Vic.

Schodde, R. and Tidemann, S. C. (eds), 1986, *Reader's Digest Complete Book of Australian Birds,* 2nd ed. Sydney

Slater, P., Slater, P. and Slater, R., 2003, *The Slater Field Guide to Australian Birds,* Reed New Holland, Sydney

MAGAZINES

The Bird Observer
quarterly journal of Bird Observers Club of Australia (BOCA)
PO Box 185, Nunawading, Vic 3131
boca@ozemail.com.au

Wingspan
quarterly journal of Birds Australia
415 Riversdale Rd, Hawthorn East Vic 3123
mail@birdsaustralia.com.au

WEBSITES

ABC Science Online
http://www2.abc.net.au/science/birds/

Australian Bird Count (ABC)
www.abc.net.au/birds

Australasian Raptor Association
http://www.ausraptor.org.au

Bird Observers Club of Australia
www.birdobservers.org.au

Birds Australia
www.birdsaustralia.com.au

Birds Australia Parrot Association
http://www.tasweb.com.au/bapa/

Cumberland Bird Observers Club
http://www.cboc.org.au

The Australian Bird Study Association
http://www.absa.asn.au

The Australasian Wader Studies Group
http://www.tasweb.com.au/awsg/index.htm

Index

bold = main entry